A Beginner's Explanation of Living Trusts and Estate Planning

How to Save Money on Probate & Taxes, Explore
Inheritance Planning, Understand How to Protect
Your Assets & Safeguard Your Legacy

George Munson

GL Digital Publishing LLC

A BEGINNER'S EXPLANATION OF LIVING TRUSTS AND ESTATE...

First edition 2024

With all my love to
Nora, Jaime, and Eli

Contents

Introduction

Estate planning can be intimidating. You sit at your kitchen table, papers strewn everywhere, trying to make sense of all the legal terms. Words like "probate" and "trustee" jump out at you, and the fear of making a costly mistake looms large. You may be navigating a maze with no clear path. You're not alone; many people feel this when first encountering estate planning. The anxiety and confusion are natural, but they don't have to hold you back.

I understand these struggles because I've seen them firsthand. My passion for helping adults navigate the complexities of estate planning has driven me to write this book.

Everyone deserves clear, actionable guidance. I aim to demystify the process and empower you with the knowledge you need to protect your assets and legacy.

This book's primary purpose is clear and straightforward: to make estate planning accessible to everyone. It aims to remove the mystery and complexity, helping you to control your financial future. Whether you're new to this process or have some experience, you'll find valuable insights and practical advice here.

The confusion surrounding estate planning is widespread. Many people need help figuring out where to start or feel overwhelmed by the jargon. The fear of making a mistake can be paralyzing. This book addresses these challenges head-on, guiding you through each step with clarity and confidence.

This book is divided into easy-to-follow sections. It starts by explaining living trusts and how they can help you avoid probate. You'll also learn about common legal challenges and tax implications. Each chapter builds on the last, ensuring you gain a comprehensive understanding. The book is structured to provide a step-by-step guide from understanding the basics to creating a comprehensive estate plan.

By reading this book, you'll reap several key benefits. You'll learn how to save money on taxes and probate. You'll understand how to draft crucial documents and gain peace of mind about your financial future. This knowledge will empower you to make informed decisions about your estate and legacy.

Throughout this journey, you'll grow in understanding and confidence. The book equips you to make decisions that reflect your wishes and protect your loved ones. It dispels myths, such as the idea that estate planning is only for the wealthy. No matter your income level, this book provides solutions tailored to your needs. I designed the book to be accessible and beneficial for everyone, regardless of their financial status.

It's essential to set realistic expectations. Following the guidance within these pages' guidance, you can establish a vital living trust and create a comprehensive estate plan. You'll gain the tools to make the right decisions for you and your family.

Engagement with the content is vital. The book includes activities and real-life examples to help you apply the concepts to your circumstances. By actively participating, you'll gain a more in-depth understanding and ensure the knowledge sticks.

It is crucial to get an early start on your estate planning journey. Regardless of your current life stage, taking action now will bring peace of mind and security for the future. Please start planning before it's too late.

Let me leave you with this encouraging thought: You have the power to take control of your estate planning journey. With the right tools and guidance, you can secure your future and ensure your wishes are honored. This book will be your guide, helping you navigate the complexities with confidence and ease. Together, let's take the first step toward protecting your legacy.

Chapter One

Understanding the Basics of Estate Planning

When considering the future, think about the legacy you'll leave behind. How will your assets be distributed, and who will manage your affairs when you can no longer do so? These questions often create a murky realm of legal jargon and unfamiliar processes. For many, estate planning conjures images of convoluted legal meetings, paperwork, and unforeseen expenses. Yet, the truth is that estate planning is an essential part of securing your financial future and ensuring your wishes are honored. It is not merely a tool for the wealthy or older people; it is a practical necessity for anyone with assets, dependents, or specific desires for their legacy.

A Beginner's Guide to Estate Planning

Estate planning is the deliberate process of organizing your assets and affairs to ensure they are managed and distributed according to your wishes after death. At its core, it protects your legacy and provides a structured asset management and distribution approach. This planning is crucial in safeguarding your possessions and ensuring a smooth transfer to your beneficiaries, minimizing potential disputes and legal challenges.

For many, the thought of their possessions being mismanaged or going to unintended recipients is unsettling. A well-crafted estate plan prevents such outcomes, allowing you to designate who receives what and when.

The benefits of organizing an estate plan extend beyond merely distributing assets. It provides financial security for your loved ones, reducing the legal hurdles they might face. One of the primary advantages is the avoidance of probate—a lengthy, costly legal process of validating a will. Probate can drain an estate's value and delay asset distribution, causing frustration and financial strain for your heirs. By planning effectively, you can also reduce estate taxes, preserving more of your wealth for your beneficiaries. These strategies ensure that your estate transitions seamlessly without legal and tax implications.

Consider the consequences of not having an estate plan. Families often face inheritance disputes, leading to fractured relationships. Lengthy probate processes can deplete an estate's value, leaving less for intended beneficiaries. Without clear directives, your assets may end up with unintended recipients, contrary to your wishes.

These pitfalls underscore the importance of planning and provide emotional and financial peace of mind. Knowing that your affairs are in order alleviates stress and uncertainty, allowing you to focus on personal goals and aspirations.

Estate planning also aligns with achieving personal goals, such as charitable giving. By including planned bequests, you can support causes you care about, leaving a meaningful impact. Many misunderstand estate planning, assuming it's only for the wealthy or elderly. In reality, it is vital for all income levels and especially for young families. It ensures that your children are cared for and your assets are protected, regardless of your financial status.

The core components of an estate plan include wills and trusts, which outline how and to whom to distribute your assets. Powers of attorney appoint trusted individuals to make decisions if you become incapacitated. These elements work together to create a comprehensive plan that reflects your wishes and secures your legacy.

Demystifying Legal Jargon

Navigating the intricacies of estate planning can feel like deciphering a foreign language. Terms such as "probate," "fiduciary," and "trustee" often lead to confusion. Yet, they are fundamental to understanding the future management of your estate. Probate, for instance, refers to the legal process of validating a will, which can be costly and time-consuming. By understanding probate, you can appreciate why many seek to avoid it through alternative strategies.

Conversely, a fiduciary is someone entrusted with managing assets for another's benefit, highlighting the importance of trust and responsibility in estate planning. Similarly, a beneficiary is an individual or entity entitled to receive assets from your estate, underscoring the need to designate who you wish to inherit your possessions. A trustee, meanwhile, is responsible for administering a trust, ensuring that your intentions are honored and assets managed according to your plans.

To provide clarity, consider the role of an executor during probate proceedings. The executor, appointed in your will, carries out your wishes, managing estate assets and paying debts. This role contrasts with a trustee, who oversees a trust independently of probate, often providing a more streamlined asset distribution.

Understanding the difference between revocable and irrevocable trusts is also crucial. As the name suggests, a revocable trust can be altered during your lifetime, offering flexibility without immediate tax benefits. In contrast, an irrevocable trust provides tax advantages but cannot be easily changed. Both serve unique purposes, allowing for tailored estate planning strategies.

A glossary of terms, organized alphabetically, can be an invaluable resource for this process. Such a glossary offers short definitions and examples, facilitating a more in-depth understanding of estate planning language. For instance, distinguishing between an executor and a trustee helps clarify roles and responsibilities. At the same time, understanding estate taxes versus inheritance taxes highlights potential financial implications for your heirs.

It's also vital to comprehend terms like "fiduciary duty," which stresses the legal obligation to act in another's best interest, and "testamentary trust," established posthumously via a will. Recognizing the distinction between a grantor, who establishes a trust, and a settlor, who funds it, further enriches your grasp of estate planning documents.

Legal jargon often appears in trust agreements and wills, where precise language dictates the distribution of assets and powers granted to fiduciaries. Sample clauses might include directives for asset allocation or stipulations for managing funds, each crafted to ensure unambiguous interpretation and execution. When deciphering such language, consider consulting legal dictionaries or seeking professional advice to enhance your comprehension and ensure your estate plan reflects your intentions accurately. Understanding probate's implications—its potential to delay and deplete an estate—reinforces the value of planning. Trustees play a crucial role in this context, tasked with managing trust assets and adhering to your directives. Selecting a trustee demands careful consideration, balancing trustworthiness with financial acumen to safeguard your estate's future.

What You Need to Know about Probate vs. Non-Probate Assets

Understanding the distinction between probate and non-probate assets is a cornerstone of effective estate planning. Probate assets require court oversight to transfer them to beneficiaries after your death. This category typically includes real estate solely in the decedent's name and personal possessions without designated beneficiaries. When such assets go through probate, they become subject to public record, potentially incurring significant legal fees and delays. The process involves validating the will, settling debts, and distributing the remaining assets. This effort can be time-consuming and costly, often depleting the estate's value before reaching the intended heirs.

Conversely, non-probate assets bypass this legal process, allowing for a more streamlined and private transfer to beneficiaries. Joint tenancy properties, where ownership automatically transfers to the surviving owner, exemplify this category. Similarly, life insurance policies with named beneficiaries ensure direct payment without court intervention.

Understanding the distinctions between these asset types can significantly influence your estate planning strategies. By designating beneficiaries on accounts and forming joint ownership where appropriate, you can minimize probate costs and expedite the transfer process.

Consider practical examples to clarify the management of these assets. Transfer-on-death (TOD) accounts and payable-on-death (POD) bank accounts offer straightforward mechanisms for asset transfer. With these arrangements, the account automatically transfers to the named beneficiary upon the holder's death, sidestepping probate entirely. Such strategies save time and resources and ensure their heirs promptly receive their inheritance. These examples illustrate the importance of meticulous planning and clear beneficiary designations. By recognizing these asset types and their implications, you can craft an estate plan that honors your wishes while preserving your estate's value for your loved ones.

An Overview of Essential Estate Planning Documents

In estate planning, certain documents stand as pillars, supporting the structure of your financial legacy. The last will, trust documents, and durable power of attorney are central to this framework. These documents act as the blueprint for your estate, directing how your assets are managed and distributed. The last will is the most familiar. It outlines who will inherit your property and possessions. This document is paramount, as it directly reflects your wishes and ensures that your beneficiaries receive what you intend. Without a will, the distribution of your assets falls to state laws, which may not align with your desires.

Trust documents, on the other hand, serve a dual function. They allocate assets during your lifetime and extend their influence beyond, often bypassing the probate process. The tailoring of trusts can meet specific needs for tax reduction, asset protection, or long-term management. With trust documents, you appoint a trustee who manages the assets on behalf of your beneficiaries, providing a layer of oversight and continuity that a simple will cannot. The durable power of attorney is equally crucial. It grants a trusted individual the authority to make financial decisions on your behalf if you become incapacitated. Doing so ensures that your affairs continue smoothly without court intervention.

The crafting of these documents requires adherence to legal requirements. Every state has its regulations, which may include witness signatures and notarization to validate the documents' legality. These requirements safeguard against disputes and ensure the documents reflect your true intentions. Understanding these specifics is vital, as failing to comply can render your documents void or open to legal challenges.

Regularly updating your documents is also essential. Life changes—such as marriage, divorce, the birth of a child, or the acquisition of new assets—necessitate revisions to keep your estate plan current. Similarly, changes in law can impact the validity of your documents. Staying informed about these changes and consulting legal professionals can help maintain the integrity of your estate plan.

Estate planning is not a one-time task but an ongoing process. It adapts to your evolving life circumstances, ensuring your wishes always align with your current situation. Engaging with these documents proactively, rather than reactively, provides peace of mind. You can rest assured that your affairs are in order, regardless of life's uncertainties. This proactive approach is not just about protecting assets; it's about preserving the legacy you wish to leave behind. Understanding and utilizing these documents effectively lays a solid foundation for your estate, ensuring your values and intentions are honored.

Common Mistakes in Estate Planning and How to Avoid Them

In estate planning, seemingly minor oversights can lead to significant complications. A prevalent mistake is the need to update estate plans regularly. Life is dynamic, marked by changes such as births, deaths, marriages, and divorces. These events necessitate reevaluating your estate documents to ensure they reflect your current intentions. With regular updates, updated plans can result in unintended asset distribution, potentially causing distress and conflict among your heirs. Set reminders for periodic reviews, perhaps annually or after significant life changes, to align your estate plan with your present wishes and circumstances.

Another often overlooked aspect is accounting for digital assets. In an increasingly digital world, your estate likely includes more than tangible items. Digital assets, such as online accounts, social media profiles, and digital currencies, hold sentimental and financial value. Failing to include these in your estate plan can lead to complications for your executors and beneficiaries. To circumvent this, maintain an inventory of your digital assets and include instructions for accessing and managing them. Consider appointing a digital executor to handle these affairs, ensuring your digital legacy is preserved and transferred according to your wishes.

Real-life case studies provide illuminating insights into the consequences of these common missteps. Take, for instance, the scenario of overlooking a beneficiary designation on a retirement account. Despite the individual's intention to update this to reflect changes in their family structure, the oversight led to an unintended relative receiving the funds, resulting in family discord. Similarly, consider an estate that inadvertently entered into probate due to an outdated will. Regularly checking for needed updates would have avoided this situation. These cases underscore the importance of vigilance and proactive management in estate planning.

Professional guidance offers invaluable support in navigating these complexities. Estate attorneys and financial advisors bring expertise and experience that can help you avoid costly errors. They can provide insights tailored to your circumstances, ensuring that your estate plan's comprehensive aspects reflect current laws. By consulting professionals, you reduce the risk of overlooked details and enhance the robustness of your estate.

In conclusion, estate planning is a nuanced task that requires ongoing attention and adjustment. By setting regular reviews and incorporating all aspects of your life, including digital assets, you safeguard against common pitfalls. Involving knowledgeable advisors further fortifies your plan, providing peace of mind that your wishes will be honored and your legacy preserved. Taking these proactive steps ensures that your estate plan reflects your intentions, offering clarity and assurance to those you leave behind.

Chapter Two

A Comprehensive Introduction to Living Trusts

You're sitting at your dining table, contemplating what will happen to your cherished belongings and assets after you're gone. Your decisions now will echo into the future, affecting your loved ones for years. It's a daunting thought, but there's a tool designed to simplify this complex task: the living trust. While many are familiar with a will, the living trust remains an enigma to some. Yet, it offers unique benefits that can transform the management of your estate.

The Difference Between a Will and a Living Trust

A will is a legal document that outlines the distribution of your assets after your death. It designates beneficiaries and, in some cases, guardians for minor children. They will only take effect upon your passing, offering a straightforward yet crucial function in estate planning. It's generally less expensive and easier to create, making it accessible for many. However, the simplicity of a will comes with certain limitations, particularly regarding probate—a court-supervised process required to validate the will and distribute assets. This process can be lengthy, potentially taking several months to several years, costly, often involving legal fees, and public, potentially subjecting your estate to public scrutiny and delays.

Unlike a will that only takes effect after passing, a living trust operates during your lifetime. It continues to manage your assets after your death. It empowers you to transfer ownership of your property to a trustee, who manages these assets for your benefit and, ultimately, for your beneficiaries. The essential advantage of a living trust is its ability to bypass probate entirely, ensuring a private and efficient transfer of assets. This trust gives you significant control and flexibility in managing your investments, allowing you to make changes as circumstances evolve, thereby putting you in the driver's seat of your estate planning.

One of a revocable living trust's most attractive features is its flexibility. As the grantor, you retain control over the trust's assets. You can modify or revoke the trust at any time during your lifetime. This adaptability is invaluable, especially when dealing with changing family dynamics such as divorce, remarriage, or financial situations like a sudden windfall or a business venture. On the other hand, a will is generally irrevocable once you pass away, meaning no one can change its terms. Contesting a will can only take place under specific legal grounds.

Consider practical scenarios to understand when each tool might be preferable. Suppose you're a parent with young children; a will can appoint guardians and ensure the distribution of your assets according to your wishes. However, a living trust might offer a seamless transition if you own multiple properties or have complex financial assets. It provides ongoing management and can automatically pass control to a successor trustee if you become incapacitated. This feature makes a living trust especially valuable for those seeking continued oversight and protection of their estate.

To illustrate, imagine a family with a substantial investment portfolio. By placing these assets in a living trust, they can ensure that the investments are managed without interruption, even if the primary trustee cannot oversee them due to health issues. In contrast, a more straightforward estate with fewer assets might rely on a will to ensure clarity and directness in asset distribution. Each tool serves its purpose, and understanding their differences empowers you to make informed decisions about your estate planning strategy.

Demystifying the Basics of a Living Trust

A living trust offers several benefits that make it an attractive option for those seeking a streamlined approach to estate planning. One of the most significant advantages is the avoidance of probate; unlike validating a will, through a lengthy and often public legal process, assets held in a living trust can be transferred directly to beneficiaries without court intervention. Doing so saves time, reduces costs, and maintains the privacy of your estate. Your assets' details and distribution remain confidential and protected from public record. Moreover, a living trust provides remarkable flexibility in managing your estate. As the trustor, you retain control over the trust's contents and can adjust the terms as needed throughout your lifetime. This adaptability is particularly beneficial if your financial situation or family dynamics change. Continuous management is another critical feature. Should you become incapacitated, a successor trustee you've designated can manage the trust's assets seamlessly, ensuring that your affairs remain in order without delay or disruption.

Asset management takes on a structured and secure format in a living trust. A trustee manages assets placed within the trust and oversees them to benefit the beneficiaries. This arrangement provides robust protection for your assets, shielding them from potential mismanagement or external claims. The ease of transfer to beneficiaries is another compelling aspect. Upon your passing, the trustee executes the distribution of assets according to the trust's directives, ensuring that your wishes are honored efficiently. This process eliminates the delays commonly associated with probate, allowing beneficiaries to receive their inheritance promptly. The trust's structure also offers protection against creditors, mainly when assets are held in an irrevocable format, adding a layer of security to your estate and instilling confidence in your estate planning decisions.

Understanding the roles of the key parties involved in a living trust is vital for informed decision-making. The trustor, also known as the grantor or settlor, is the individual who creates the trust and transfers assets into it. As the trustor, you can outline the terms of the trust and make any necessary changes during your lifetime. The trustee you appoint manages the trust's assets according to your instructions. This role requires diligence and integrity, as the trustee must act in the best interests of the beneficiaries.

Beneficiaries are the individuals or entities entitled to receive the trust's assets. The trust defines their rights by the trust's terms, which specify when and how distributions are to occur. Together, these parties form the foundation of the living trust, each playing a vital role in its operation and success, and by understanding these roles, you can feel more knowledgeable and confident in your estate planning decisions.

Creating a living trust involves several steps, beginning with a clear understanding of your objectives and the assets you wish to include. You will need to draft a trust document that outlines the trust's terms, including the designation of a trustee and successor trustee. This document is the blueprint for the trust's operation, detailing how assets must be managed and distributed. In establishing the trust, you must transfer ownership of your chosen assets into the trust, which may involve re-titling property and updating account information. This step is critical to ensuring that the trust functions as intended, as any assets not formally transferred will remain subject to probate. As you proceed, consider consulting legal and financial professionals who can provide guidance and ensure that your living trust aligns with your estate planning goals.

Making the Right Choice between Revocable vs. Irrevocable Trusts

Understanding the nuanced differences between revocable versus irrevocable trusts is crucial in estate planning. A revocable trust, often called a living trust, offers flexibility and control. You can modify or revoke it at any time during your lifetime. This adaptability is advantageous for those anticipating asset changes or family dynamics. However, this flexibility comes at a cost; assets in a revocable trust are not shielded from creditors and do not offer significant tax advantages.

In contrast, an irrevocable trust involves permanently transferring ownership of assets to the trust. Once established, beneficiaries must consent to changes. This rigidity provides robust asset protection and potential tax benefits, making it a strategic choice for those who shield assets from creditors or minimize estate taxes.

The decision between these trust types involves weighing their respective advantages and disadvantages. Revocable trusts provide ease of management, allowing you to retain control over your assets. They are adequate for estate planning purposes but improve asset protection. On the other hand, irrevocable trusts, while inflexible, offer more robust protection against creditors and can facilitate significant tax savings. For example, assets transferred to an irrevocable trust are generally not included in your estate for tax purposes, potentially reducing your estate's tax liability. These trusts can also help you qualify for Medicaid by removing assets from your ownership, a critical consideration for long-term care planning.

When deciding which trust aligns with your goals, consider your need for control versus your desire for protection. Ask yourself about your long-term financial objectives and any concerns about potential creditors.

If you prioritize flexibility and foresee changes in your life circumstances, a revocable trust may suit you best. Conversely, if safeguarding assets and reducing taxes are your primary concerns, an irrevocable trust might be the better option. For instance, a young family with evolving financial needs might benefit from the adaptability of a revocable trust, allowing for adjustments as the family grows. Meanwhile, individuals with substantial assets or those seeking to protect wealth from potential litigation might lean towards an irrevocable trust.

Consider the practical applications of these trusts. A revocable trust aids in managing assets through life's transitions without losing control. It ensures continuity and ease of amendment, accommodating changes in family situations or asset holdings. An irrevocable trust, however, is well-suited for estate tax planning and asset protection. It effectively removes assets from your taxable estate, offering security against creditors. Each trust type serves distinct purposes, and understanding these can guide you in selecting the trust that best meets your specific needs and priorities.

How to Set Up a Living Trust

Creating a living trust requires careful planning and attention to detail. Begin by gathering the necessary documents. Doing so includes a comprehensive list of assets, titles, deeds, and financial statements. These documents provide the foundation for your trust, offering a clear view of what you intend to protect and manage. Next, draft the trust document, a legal instrument that outlines the terms of the trust. This document specifies the trustee, successor trustee, and beneficiaries, alongside any conditions you wish to impose. It's crucial to fund the trust adequately.

Funding the trust means transferring ownership of assets into the trust, a step often overlooked yet vital for the trust's efficacy. If assets remain outside the trust, they may still be subject to probate, defeating one of the primary purposes of establishing a trust. Asset titling is essential to ensure all property is in the trust. The consequences of an unfunded trust are significant, potentially leaving your estate vulnerable to legal proceedings and unintended asset distribution.

Choosing a trustee and beneficiary is a crucial decision. The trustee manages the trust's assets, acting in the best interests of the beneficiaries. Trustworthiness and financial acumen are critical qualities to consider when selecting a trustee. Beneficiaries, on the other hand, are those who will benefit from the trust and receive distributions as outlined in the trust document. Listing and valuing assets accurately is another crucial step. Valuing involves assessing your property's current and potential future value, providing a realistic picture of your estate's worth. It is necessary to consider legal formalities and state requirements, as they vary across jurisdictions. Compliance with these laws ensures the trust's validity and enforceability.

Consulting with legal counsel is highly recommended when setting up a living trust. Estate attorneys bring expertise to the process, helping to navigate complex legal landscapes and avoid common pitfalls, such as improperly drafted documents or unclear terms. Their guidance can help tailor the trust to your needs, enhancing its effectiveness. A living trust offers strategic advantages that can enhance estate planning outcomes. It protects your assets from potential disputes and creditors, ensuring efficient management and distribution. Trusts can prevent family conflicts by clearly outlining your wishes, reducing the likelihood of disagreements among heirs.

Despite these benefits, some may perceive trusts as complex or costly. However, the long-term savings and peace of mind often outweigh initial expenses. Many misunderstand the control retained over assets in a living trust, mistakenly believing it relinquishes ownership. In truth, a revocable trust allows you to maintain control with the flexibility to amend its terms. To streamline the trust setup process, organize your financial records meticulously. Clear communication with beneficiaries is also essential, ensuring they understand their roles and expectations. This transparency fosters trust and cooperation, paving the way for a smoother transition of assets.

Real-Life Scenarios about Choosing the Right Trust for Your Needs

Let's consider a family dynamic many might recognize: the blended family. Imagine a couple where each partner has children from previous marriages. They face the challenge of ensuring all children feel equally valued while protecting the inheritance each parent wishes to leave. A trust tailored for a blended family can offer a solution. It allows the couple to define specific terms that cater to each child's needs, ensuring fairness and clarity. The family can prevent potential conflicts and misinterpretations by establishing such trust. However, this requires careful management and regular updates to reflect changing family dynamics.

Now consider a scenario involving a special needs child. Parents often worry about securing their child's future care and financial stability. A special needs trust can provide the necessary support. This trust ensures that the child receives financial assistance without jeopardizing eligibility for government benefits. The parents can appoint a trustee to manage the funds, safeguarding the child's interests. It's a strategy that provides peace of mind to parents, knowing their child will have the resources needed without the risk of losing crucial benefits. Such a trust requires precise structuring to comply with legal requirements and maximize support.

The outcomes of these scenarios highlight effective asset management strategies. Trusts for blended families foster equity and transparency, reducing potential familial discord. Meanwhile, special needs trusts secure financial resources while preserving benefit eligibility. Yet, these scenarios reveal challenges, such as navigating complex family relationships or ensuring compliance with evolving legal standards. These challenges necessitate ongoing attention and adaptation to maintain the trust's effectiveness.

When deciding on the appropriate trust, consider frameworks that evaluate family dynamics and financial objectives. Begin by assessing your family's unique needs and relationships. Are there specific concerns or goals you wish to address? Next, examine your financial landscape. What assets need protection, and what future expenses should you plan for? You create a tool that serves your situation by aligning your trust with these factors. Customization plays a crucial role in tailoring trusts. You can add special clauses, like contingencies for educational expenses or medical needs, and adjust beneficiary provisions to reflect personal circumstances.

Overcoming the Common Objections of Why Trusts Are Worth It

When considering a living trust, you might encounter skepticism rooted in misconceptions about its complexity and cost. Many believe that trusts are reserved for the wealthy or involve intricate legal processes that are daunting to navigate. In reality, while setting up a trust does require an initial investment of time and resources, the long-term benefits often far outweigh these concerns. A living trust can offer substantial cost savings by avoiding the probate process, which can be expensive and time-consuming. By sidestepping probate, you save on legal fees and expedite the distribution of assets to your beneficiaries, fulfilling your wishes without unnecessary delay.

Concerns about control and flexibility also arise when discussing trusts. A common misconception is that once you place assets in a trust, you lose control over them. However, you maintain complete authority over your assets with a revocable living trust. You can adjust the trust's terms, add or remove assets, and even dissolve the trust altogether if your circumstances change. This level of control provides peace of mind, knowing that your estate plan can evolve alongside your life.

To illustrate the practical benefits of a living trust, consider the testimonials from individuals who have experienced these advantages firsthand. One individual shared how her mother's estate bypassed the lengthy probate process, allowing her to receive her inheritance swiftly and without the public scrutiny associated with probate. Another individual highlighted the tax efficiencies achieved through a properly structured trust, reducing the family's tax burden and preserving more wealth for future generations. These real-life examples underscore the tangible benefits of a well-planned trust.

The long-term peace of mind a trust provides is invaluable. Knowing that managing your estate and protecting your beneficiaries according to your specifications helps alleviate anxiety. A trust ensures a seamless transition of assets, reducing family conflicts and providing clarity to all involved. Addressing these common objections and showcasing the compelling advantages makes it clear why a living trust is a powerful tool in estate planning. Trusts offer a unique combination of security, control, and efficiency, making them a worthwhile consideration for anyone seeking to protect their legacy.

Chapter Three

Protecting Your Assets and Beneficiaries

Envision standing at the edge of a vast, uncharted territory, representing your life's work and accumulated wealth. You want to ensure it remains safe, grows, and passes on to those you care about. Asset allocation serves as the map guiding you through this territory, helping you strategically manage your resources. In estate planning, asset allocation distributes your investments across different categories to balance risk and return. Diversification, a cornerstone of this practice, involves spreading investments across various asset types to mitigate risk. Not putting all your eggs in one basket protects your assets from market fluctuations, ensuring long-term growth and stability. This strategic approach enhances financial security and aligns with your broader estate planning goals.

Creating a well-thought-out asset strategy is crucial for achieving your financial objectives. Begin by setting clear short-term and long-term goals. Short-term objectives include building an emergency fund or saving for a family vacation. At the same time, long-term goals could focus on retirement or funding your children's education. Evaluate the liquidity of your assets and how convertible they are into cash without losing value. Liquid assets, like stocks and bonds, provide flexibility.

In contrast, less liquid assets, such as real estate, may require more time to access. Shielding your assets from creditors is another vital consideration. Legal structures, like limited liability companies (LLCs), can offer protection by separating personal and business assets, reducing exposure to potential claims. Preserving wealth for future generations requires careful planning, ensuring that your legacy endures.

Real estate often emerges as a reliable long-term investment when allocating different asset types. Property can appreciate over time, providing both income and security. On the other hand, stocks offer growth potential, allowing you to capitalize on market opportunities. Balancing these asset types within your portfolio helps you achieve a harmonious blend of security and growth. The role of legal structures in protecting your assets is vital. LLCs and family limited partnerships (FLPs) are barriers to safeguarding your wealth from external threats. An LLC offers liability protection, while an FLP allows for the efficient transfer of business interests, often at discounted values. These structures protect assets and facilitate seamless transitions across generations, ensuring your estate plan remains robust and effective.

Create Your Asset Allocation Strategy

To help you navigate your asset allocation, consider this exercise:

- **Inventory Your Assets:** List all assets, including their current value and liquidity.

- **Define Your Goals:** Identify both short-term and long-term financial objectives.

- **Assess Risk Tolerance:** Determine your comfort level with risk, considering your investment horizon.

- **Choose Asset Classes:** Decide how much of your portfolio to allocate to real estate, stocks, bonds, and other assets.

- **Implement Legal Protections:** Explore LLCs or FLPs to shield assets from creditors and optimize tax efficiency.

By engaging with this exercise, you develop a personalized strategy that aligns with your estate planning goals, setting the stage for a secure and prosperous future.

How to Transfer Assets to Fund Your Trust

Transferring assets into a living trust is critical in ensuring your estate plan functions as intended. This process, known as funding the trust, involves re-titling holdings so that the trust owns them rather than you. Begin with real estate, a significant component of many estates. To transfer real estate into a trust, you must sign and record a deed that transfers your property interest to the trust. This step is crucial, as failure to re-title real estate means it could remain subject to probate, defeating the trust's primary purpose. Similarly, transferring bank accounts requires contacting your financial institutions to update account ownership to the trust's name, ensuring the management of these funds according to the trust's directives without interruption.

A diverse array of assets can be included in your trust, each requiring specific actions to ensure proper transfer. Stocks and bonds, for example, must have their ownership re-titled to reflect your trust as the new owner. Doing so often involves working with your brokerage to update records and ensuring the management of these investments within the trust's framework. Personal property, such as valuable collections or vehicles, can also be transferred. Transferring this involves drafting a general transfer document that lists and affirms the trust's ownership of these items.

Adequately funding your trust is crucial, as incomplete transfers can lead to assets bypassing the trust, thereby undergoing probate. This oversight can result in unintended delays and costs, undermining trusts' efficiency and privacy.

To aid in this process:

- Consider a checklist to ensure comprehensive asset transfer.

- Start by confirming that all real estate deeds have been updated and recorded under the trust's name.

- Verify that bank accounts and investment portfolios reflect the trust's ownership.

Updating life insurance and retirement account beneficiary designations is important to align with your estate plan. To maintain the integrity of your trust, regularly revisit this checklist, particularly after significant life changes. This diligence ensures that your trust operates as intended, safeguarding your estate and honoring your wishes.

How to Choose and Appoint a Trustee

Selecting a trustee is a pivotal decision in establishing a trust. This individual or entity manages trust assets and ensures they follow your directives. Primarily, a trustee upholds a fiduciary duty to beneficiaries, always acting in their best interest. Upholding involves:

- Overseeing the administration of trust assets.

- Making informed decisions about investments.

- Ensuring that the distribution of assets aligns with the trust's terms.

The trustee must manage these tasks with prudence and integrity, maintaining transparency and accountability throughout the process. Understanding this role's gravity is crucial as it involves financial oversight and adherence to your wishes.

When choosing a trustee, consider several criteria to ensure the individual is well-equipped for the task. Trustworthiness is paramount, as this person will handle assets and potentially sensitive information. Evaluate personal relationships; sometimes, a family member might seem an ideal choice due to familiarity, but they may lack the objective distance required for fair administration. Professional expertise in financial management can be equally important, especially for complex estates. A trustee with solid financial acumen can navigate market shifts and protect the trust's value. Balancing these factors helps ensure your trustee can effectively manage the trust while honoring your intentions.

Compensation is another aspect to consider. Trustee compensation is average for their service, with structures varying based on the trust's size and complexity. These fees can impact the overall value of the trust, so it's essential to understand the implications. Clear agreements about compensation prevent misunderstandings and help maintain trust between parties. Consider how trustee fees might affect your beneficiaries' inheritance and weigh this against the benefits of professional expertise.

Potential conflicts of interest can arise if a trustee stands to gain from trust decisions. To mitigate these risks, clearly communicate roles and responsibilities from the outset. Implementing checks and balances, such as appointing co-trustees or requiring third-party oversight for significant decisions, can ensure accountability. These measures help maintain the trust's integrity and protect the beneficiaries' interests, ensuring the trustee operates impartially and fairly.

The Responsibilities and Selection of a Trustee and Their Role

Imagine entrusting someone with the keys to your kingdom, where they're responsible for safeguarding and distributing your life's work according to your wishes. This responsibility is the role of a trustee, a position that requires both diligence and integrity. A trustee's primary duty is to manage the trust's assets effectively, ensuring they are preserved and grown to benefit the beneficiaries. This duty involves making informed investment decisions, maintaining accurate records, and complying with relevant legal and tax obligations. Beyond management, the trustee must distribute assets to beneficiaries as specified in the trust document. This task requires precision and impartiality, as it directly affects the financial future of those involved.

Selecting a trustee is a decision that demands careful consideration. It would be best if you looked for someone with strong financial acumen, capable of navigating the complexities of asset management. This individual must also exhibit impartiality, treating all beneficiaries fairly and without bias, ensuring that personal relationships do not cloud their judgment. Reliability is another critical trait; the trustee must be steadfast, fulfilling their duties consistently and with integrity. This role isn't just about managing money—it's about maintaining trust and upholding the values you wish to embody in your legacy.

However, being a trustee has its challenges. Trustees may face conflicts among beneficiaries, differing interpretations of trust terms, or fluctuations in market conditions affecting the trust's assets. Clear communication and transparency are essential to address these issues. Keeping beneficiaries informed about decisions and changes can prevent misunderstandings and foster trust. It's also vital for trustees to seek professional advice when necessary, ensuring their actions align with legal requirements and best practices. By maintaining open lines of communication and adhering to the trust's directives, trustees can navigate these challenges, ensuring the trust operates smoothly and following your wishes.

Protecting Minor Beneficiaries with Guardians and Trusts

When considering the future of minor beneficiaries, guardianship becomes a cornerstone of their financial and personal welfare. Legal and financial are two main types of guardianship. A legal guardian assumes responsibility for the child's day-to-day care, including education, healthcare, and general well-being decisions. In contrast, a financial guardian focuses solely on managing the minor's financial affairs; they ensure wise asset preservation and utilization until the child reaches adulthood. The role of a guardian is both a privilege and a responsibility, requiring a deep commitment to the child's best interests.

Trusts for minors are another crucial component in safeguarding their financial future. Establishing a minor's trust allows you to set specific terms for how and when the child will receive their inheritance. This structure prevents the child from squandering their assets too early, providing financial security through structured distributions. For instance, you might arrange for funds to be released at certain ages or upon reaching specific milestones, such as completing higher education. Trusts offer flexibility and control, enabling you to tailor the financial support to the child's needs and maturity.

Legal considerations in appointing guardians or setting up trusts for minors are paramount. Courts often oversee guardianship to ensure the chosen guardian is suitable and committed to the child's welfare. Doing so involves legal documentation that outlines the guardian's responsibilities and the conditions of their appointment. Similarly, setting up a trust for a minor requires precise legal documentation to define the trust's terms and the trustee's duties. These legal frameworks ensure that someone upholds your intentions for the minor's care and financial security.

Consider the case of a family who established a trust for their young child. The parents included provisions for educational expenses, ensuring funds were available for college tuition. This planning secured the child's education and relieved financial pressures on the family. In another example, a successful guardianship arrangement involved a legal guardian working closely with a financial guardian to balance personal care with financial management, illustrating the effectiveness of this dual approach. These scenarios highlight the importance of thoughtful planning and legal diligence in protecting minor beneficiaries.

Strategies to Streamline Asset Transfer for Avoiding Probate

People often consider probate an unavoidable hurdle in estate planning, but understanding its drawbacks reveals why many seek alternatives. The probate process is notorious for being lengthy and fraught with delays. This legal procedure can drag on for months, sometimes years, tying up assets and leaving beneficiaries in limbo. Moreover, probate is a public process, meaning your estate's details become part of the public record, exposing private family matters and financial information to anyone interested. The associated costs, including court fees and legal expenses, can further erode the estate's value, diminishing what your heirs receive.

Strategic planning is imperative to avoid these challenges. One effective method is establishing joint ownership arrangements. By holding property jointly with rights of survivorship, the asset automatically transfers to the surviving owner, bypassing probate entirely. This practice is commonly used for real estate and bank accounts, offering a straightforward solution. Similarly, designating beneficiaries on financial accounts like IRAs and life insurance policies ensures these assets are transferred directly to the named individuals, avoiding probate. These simple designations provide clarity and efficiency, securing the swift passage of assets to intended beneficiaries without judicial intervention.

Another powerful tool for avoiding probate is the Transfer-on-Death (TOD) designation. This option allows you to name a beneficiary who will inherit specific assets upon death. The beauty of TOD lies in its simplicity; it requires minimal paperwork and avoids court proceedings. Once the asset owner passes, the beneficiary must only provide a death certificate to assume ownership. This method is particularly beneficial for brokerage accounts and securities, offering a seamless transfer process. The advantages of TOD designations extend beyond efficiency, providing peace of mind by ensuring your wishes are honored promptly.

Living trusts play a central role in sidestepping probate, offering privacy and simplicity in asset distribution. By placing assets in a living trust, you retain control during your lifetime while ensuring they are managed and distributed according to your directives after death, without court involvement. Trusts protect your estate from public scrutiny and allow for a customized distribution plan, accommodating complex family dynamics or specific bequests. The streamlined nature of living trusts makes them a preferred choice for those seeking to protect their estate's integrity and ensure a smooth transition for their beneficiaries.

Navigating the Complex Tax Implications of Trusts and Taxes

Understanding how trusts are taxed is crucial in estate planning. Depending on the trust's structure, trusts can incur income taxes on earnings, either paid by the trust itself or passed to the beneficiaries. This taxation affects how much income remains for distribution. Estate taxes are another consideration. While trusts can help minimize these taxes, they must be structured correctly. Estate taxes can significantly reduce what beneficiaries receive, so planning is essential.

Exploring tax-advantaged trusts can provide solutions. Charitable remainder trusts, for instance, allow you to receive income from the trust during your lifetime, with the remaining assets going to a charity upon your death. This setup can offer income tax deductions and reduce estate taxes. Grantor-retained annuity trusts (GRATs) are another tool. They let you transfer assets to beneficiaries with minimal gift tax implications, allowing for tax-efficient wealth transfer.

Effective tax planning strategies are vital. Utilizing annual gift tax exclusions can reduce the taxable estate, allowing you to give each beneficiary a certain amount tax-free yearly. Structuring trusts for tax efficiency involves careful planning to make the most of available deductions and credits. Consulting with tax professionals is invaluable in this process. A tax advisor can guide you through the complexities of trust taxation, helping you stay informed on tax law changes that could impact your estate plan.

Consider some common tax scenarios involving trusts. An irrevocable trust, for example, removes assets from your taxable estate, potentially reducing estate taxes. However, this also means you lose control over those assets. State-specific tax laws can further complicate matters, as some states have their own estate or inheritance taxes. Understanding these nuances is crucial to ensuring your estate plan is tax-efficient. By leveraging the right strategies and seeking professional guidance, you can navigate the complexities of trust taxation and maximize the benefits for your beneficiaries.

Chapter Four

Personalized Estate Planning Strategies

A family is at dinner with a mix of biological and stepchildren, all sharing their hopes and worries about the future; a common scenario in many households today, where blended families face unique challenges in estate planning. Balancing the interests of both biological and step-family members can be complex, often requiring a thoughtful approach to ensure fairness and clarity. One crucial strategy is the use of pre-marital agreements. These agreements, which delineate the division of assets before marriage, serve as a solid foundation, reducing potential conflicts by clearly defining what belongs to whom. Another effective method is creating separate trusts for children from previous marriages, ensuring the allocation of specific assets as intended and providing peace of mind for parents and children alike.

Ensuring a fair distribution of assets in blended families can be challenging but achievable with careful planning. Life insurance can play a significant role, using it to equalize inheritances. Providing a lump sum to particular beneficiaries can balance the distribution of other assets. Establishing joint accounts with stepchildren can also foster a sense of inclusion and fairness. These accounts allow for shared financial goals and responsibilities, helping to bridge any gaps between step-siblings.

However, even with the best intentions, legal challenges can arise. Contesting wills and trusts is expected, mainly when perceived inequities exist. Disputes over guardianship of minors may also occur, especially in blended families, where multiple parties may have a vested interest in the child's welfare.

Effective communication is crucial in navigating the challenges of estate planning for blended families. Regular family meetings can provide open dialogue about inheritance plans, allowing all members to voice their expectations and concerns. This transparency can prevent misunderstandings and foster a collaborative environment. Encouraging open dialogue about expectations and concerns ensures that everyone feels heard and respected, reducing the likelihood of disputes. Carefully documenting these discussions and agreements is essential, as they serve as a reference point should conflicts arise later. By approaching estate planning with sensitivity and foresight, blended families can create a harmonious plan that respects each member's role and legacy.

Family Communication Exercise

Create a family meeting agenda to discuss estate planning. Include asset distribution, guardianship preferences, and family members' concerns. Encourage each member to prepare a list of their expectations and questions. This exercise fosters open communication and helps establish a clear understanding among all parties, paving the way for a smoother estate planning process.

Inventory and Asset Allocation for Mapping Your Estate

Taking a comprehensive inventory of your estate is a foundational step in planning. Begin by identifying and listing every asset you own to account for everything. Real estate holdings are often among the most significant assets. Carefully evaluate each property's current market value and potential appreciation. Personal property, including collections and heirlooms, must also be assessed. These items may carry both financial and sentimental value, requiring careful consideration. Financial accounts, such as savings and investment portfolios, and retirement accounts, like IRAs, form another crucial part of your inventory. Annotate each account with account numbers and current balances. Remember, digital assets and intellectual property are increasingly valuable. These include online accounts, digital currencies, and any proprietary works or trademarks you own.

Accurate asset valuation is paramount. It directly impacts your estate planning decisions, influencing tax strategies and asset distribution. Professionals should conduct real estate appraisals to ensure precision, particularly for unique or high-value properties. Similarly, appraising personal belongings might require experts, especially for rare or antique items. This accuracy provides a realistic picture of your estate's worth, informing all subsequent planning decisions. Asset allocation strategies should align with your estate planning goals. Balance tangible and intangible assets, ensuring diversity to mitigate risk. Aligning asset distribution with financial goals allows for strategic growth and wealth protection. Professional assistance can prove invaluable in this complex process. Hiring appraisers ensures accurate valuations, while financial advisors provide insights into strategic allocation. Their expertise can help navigate complex estates, offering peace of mind that your assets are managed effectively and following your wishes.

What Goals Do You Want with Your Estate Plan?

Imagine sitting quietly, contemplating the future. What do you truly desire for your estate? It's crucial to define clear objectives that reflect your values and aspirations. Perhaps you aim to preserve wealth, ensuring your hard-earned assets continue to benefit your loved ones. Consider how you might support heirs and dependents, providing them with a financial foundation. Charitable contributions, too, might play a role, allowing you to give back and leave a philanthropic legacy. Prioritizing these goals is essential. Balancing these goals against long-term visions, such as sustaining wealth across generations and securing educational funds, is necessary. Family needs often intertwine with personal desires, requiring careful deliberation.

Personal circumstances inevitably shape your estate planning objectives. A marital status change or family dynamic shift might require reevaluating priorities, ensuring your plan remains relevant. Health considerations, as you age, also influence your decisions, prompting adjustments to accommodate future care needs. To keep your estate plan on track, utilize goal-setting worksheets, which provide a structured approach to articulating and refining your objectives. However, the journey continues. Regular reviews and updates ensure your plan reflects your current intentions and adapts to new realities. This ongoing process can provide reassurance and control over your estate's future.

Special Considerations for Business Owners and Estate Planning

Imagine the day you decide to step back from your business. What happens next? Succession planning ensures your business continues smoothly, safeguarding its future and your legacy. A clear succession plan identifies potential successors, whether they're family members or trained employees. They should understand the business intricacies, ensuring stability when the time comes. Training is crucial. It prepares successors for their roles, instilling confidence in clients and employees. Evaluating your business's worth is another critical step. Accurate valuation informs your estate plan, affecting inheritance taxes and decisions about asset division. Methods vary, from market comparisons to income approaches, each offering insights into your business's value. Protecting these assets is equally important. A buy-sell agreement can facilitate a seamless transition, dictating how to transfer shares upon retirement or death. Life insurance can fund these transfers, providing liquidity and preventing financial strain. Taxes also play a pivotal role. Transferring ownership triggers considerations like gift and estate taxes. Strategies like gifting shares over time or utilizing family-limited partnerships can minimize liabilities, preserving your business's value for future generations.

Planning the Protection of Your Online Digital Assets

In today's digital age, your online presence and assets are as significant as your tangible ones. Digital assets encompass various items, from online financial accounts and social media profiles to digital currencies and intellectual properties. These assets hold monetary and sentimental value, making them crucial to modern estate planning. It is necessary to account for online accounts, such as PayPal or investment platforms, and house funds. While non-financial assets, social media profiles carry sentimental weight, preserving memories and personal connections. Recognizing the importance of these digital assets ensures they are managed and transferred according to your wishes, just like your physical estate.

Creating a digital asset plan is a proactive safeguard for your online legacy. Start by compiling an inventory of all digital assets, including login credentials and access information. This list should cover everything from email accounts to cloud storage. Designate a digital executor, a trusted individual responsible for managing these assets after your passing. This role involves overseeing access, distribution, and, if necessary, the closure of accounts. Including this in your will ensures your digital executor has the legal authority to carry out your instructions, preventing potential access issues or disputes.

Legal and privacy considerations are paramount in managing digital assets. Terms of service agreements often dictate how accounts are handled posthumously, with some platforms requiring specific documentation or procedures. Understanding these terms helps avoid complications. Protecting personal information online also remains vital. Use secure methods to store passwords and access information, minimizing the risk of unauthorized access. Discussing your wishes with an estate planner can help navigate these legal intricacies, ensuring compliance with terms and safeguarding your digital legacy.

Practical tools are available to assist in managing digital assets effectively. Digital asset management software offers a centralized platform to organize and track your online holdings. These tools often include features to document ownership and designate access rights. Online password managers are another invaluable resource. They store and encrypt login credentials, providing secure access to your accounts while simplifying management. By integrating these tools into your estate planning process, you enhance security and ensure a smooth transition of digital assets following your wishes.

Choosing Beneficiaries to Ensure Your Wishes Are Honored

Choosing beneficiaries is a critical aspect of estate planning that requires careful thought. Consider who you wish to inherit your assets, starting with immediate family members and dependents. These individuals often include spouses, children, and relatives who rely on your support. Beyond family, consider charitable organizations or foundations that align with your values. Naming such entities as beneficiaries can leave a lasting impact and help perpetuate causes vital to you. This decision should reflect your priorities and how you envision your legacy.

Equitable distribution among beneficiaries is crucial to prevent conflicts. Strive for fairness while recognizing that equal distribution may not always equate to equity. Your family dynamics play a significant role here, and addressing potential conflicts can prevent disputes later. Additional planning for special needs dependents or minors ensures they receive support without jeopardizing benefits. Consider a special needs trust or similar arrangements to secure their future. Clear communication with beneficiaries is vital. Engage in open discussions to manage expectations and avoid misunderstandings. Family meetings can facilitate these conversations, allowing all parties to express their views. Documenting your intentions clearly in estate planning documents reduces ambiguity and ensures your wishes are honored.

Beneficiary designations should remain current and relevant. Regular reviews and updates are necessary, especially after significant life events such as marriages, divorces, or childbirth. These changes can significantly impact your estate plan, and timely adjustments prevent unintended consequences. Keeping beneficiary information up-to-date ensures your estate is distributed according to your most recent wishes, protecting your assets and legacy.

Appointing Guardians for Minor Children

Choosing suitable guardians for your minor children is a decision of immense importance. These individuals will be responsible for your children's well-being, shaping their future in your absence. When evaluating potential guardians, consider their values and parenting style. Reflect on how these align with your own beliefs and how they might influence your children's development. You want someone who will honor your wishes and provide the care and guidance your children need. It's not just about who they are today but who they will be in the years to come as your children grow.

When appointing guardians, use a checklist to guide your decision. Financial stability is crucial, as guardians should be able to provide for their children without compromising their economic security. Their relationship with your children is equally important. Consider the bond they share and how this might affect the transition. Will your children feel comfortable and loved in their care? Remember to address legal considerations. Formalizing guardianship decisions in legal documents, like wills, ensures your choice is recognized and respected. Drafting guardianship clauses provides clarity, reduces the potential for disputes, and ensures your children's futures are secured as you intend.

Successful guardianship arrangements often involve establishing backup guardians. Life is unpredictable, and unforeseen circumstances can arise. Designating a secondary guardian ensures continuity in care, providing a safety net if the primary guardian cannot fulfill their role. Consider a case where a family appointed a close friend as the primary guardian, with a trusted relative as the backup. This arrangement offered peace of mind, knowing their children would be cared for by individuals familiar with their needs and family dynamics. Thoughtful planning and clear documentation enable you to make informed choices, safeguarding your children's well-being and honoring your role as a parent, even when you're no longer present.

Planning for Special Needs Beneficiaries with Trust Options and More

When planning for a special needs beneficiary's future, consider unique considerations to ensure their financial security and well-being. Eligibility for government benefits is critical, as these benefits often provide essential support. However, receiving an inheritance can inadvertently disqualify a beneficiary from these programs. Understanding long-term care needs is also necessary, as these individuals may require ongoing assistance beyond essential financial support. Establishing a framework that accommodates these needs without compromising benefits is paramount. Trust options play a significant role in this planning.

A Special Needs Trust (SNT) offers a tailored solution, allowing the setting aside assets for the beneficiary's benefit without affecting their eligibility for government aid. First-party SNTs are funded with the beneficiary's assets, often from settlements or inheritances, while family members or other benefactors fund third-party SNTs. Pooled trusts provide cost-effective management by pooling resources from multiple beneficiaries, offering professional oversight, and reducing administrative burdens. Coordinating estate plans with government benefits ensures trust funds do not interfere with eligibility. Careful attention to reporting requirements for trust income is necessary to comply with regulations and avoid jeopardizing benefits. Family members and caregivers play a vital role in this process. Appointing a knowledgeable trustee who understands the beneficiary's needs and legal obligations is crucial. Developing a comprehensive care plan that outlines the beneficiary's needs, preferences, and goals guides trustees and caregivers, ensuring continuity and quality of care.

Appointing the Right Trustee, their Roles and Responsibilities

Selecting a trustee involves more than picking a name from your contact list. The trustee's role is steeped in responsibility, requiring careful management of assets and scrupulous distribution according to your wishes. This position demands a strong understanding of financial management and a commitment to ethical considerations. Trustees must act with integrity, prioritizing the beneficiaries' interests above all else and fulfilling their fiduciary duties. This obligation means they must manage the trust's funds wisely, ensuring assets are preserved and grown where possible. Their ethical compass must guide every decision, maintaining transparency and fairness.

Choosing the right trustee is critical. You'll weigh the benefits of appointing a family member against hiring a professional trustee. Family members may deeply understand your wishes but need more financial acumen. While more costly, professional trustees offer expertise and impartiality, which can be invaluable in complex situations. Trustworthiness and financial insight are paramount. To avoid conflicts of interest, establish clear guidelines and oversight mechanisms. Co-trustees can offer balanced decision-making, providing checks and balances. A succession plan is essential. Name a successor trustee and outline legal provisions for trustee replacement, ensuring continuity if the original trustee can no longer serve.

Putting It All Together to Craft a Comprehensive Estate Plan

Constructing a well-rounded estate plan involves several vital components. At its core, a living trust or will should outline the distribution of your assets after your passing. These documents provide the foundation of your estate plan, ensuring your wishes are respected. Complementing these are powers of attorney, granting trusted individuals the authority to make financial and medical decisions if incapacitated. Healthcare directives are equally vital, detailing your preferences for medical treatment and providing guidance to healthcare providers and loved ones. Each document plays a specific role, but its true strength lies in how it integrates into a cohesive plan. Coordinating these elements ensures consistency; they must align to reflect your overall intentions.

Meeting all legal requirements is crucial. Doing so involves having documents signed, witnessed, and notarized where necessary, safeguarding against challenges. As you finalize your estate plan, follow a detailed checklist. Review each document thoroughly, ensuring they reflect your current wishes. Once finalized, sign them in the presence of witnesses if required and store them securely. Inform trusted individuals about where to find these documents. Regular updates are also vital as laws change and life events occur. Scheduling periodic reviews helps keep your plan relevant and practical, ensuring it adapts as needed.

Case Studies and Examples of Tailoring Your Estate Plan

Consider a family where both partners bring children from previous marriages. They face the challenge of creating an estate plan that ensures equity and honors each child's legacy. They opted for separate trusts, allowing each parent to safeguard assets for their biological children while maintaining family harmony. This strategy provided clarity and avoided potential disputes, illustrating the importance of tailored solutions in estate planning.

Another scenario involves a business owner planning for succession. They crafted a detailed plan involving training a successor while implementing a buy-sell agreement funded by life insurance. This approach guaranteed a smooth transition without financial strain, demonstrating the value of preparation in preserving business continuity.

Each case uncovered successes and challenges. The blended family benefited from clear communication, ensuring all members understood the plan's intentions. The business owner faced obstacles in balancing tax implications but leveraged expert advice to navigate these complexities. Practical lessons emerge from these examples:

- Maintain flexibility in adapting plans to life's changes and prioritize clear communication to prevent misunderstandings.

- Reflect on your circumstances and consider how these strategies might apply.

- Identify your goals, evaluate your family dynamics, and ensure your estate plan reflects your needs and aspirations.

Stories of What Went Wrong

Consider a family that thought they had everything covered, only to find their estate depleted by unexpected taxes. They needed to account for changes in tax law and update their estate plan over the years. This oversight led to a significant portion of their estate going to the government, much to the shock and dismay of their intended heirs. The lesson here is clear: Regular estate plan reviews are not just advisable but necessary.

Another case involved siblings embroiled in a bitter legal battle over their parents' estate. The dispute was rooted in a poorly chosen executor who lacked the skills and impartiality to manage the estate reasonably. It spiraled into costly litigation, fracturing family bonds irreparably. This scenario highlights the importance of selecting a competent and neutral executor.

These stories underscore the pitfalls of neglect and poor decision-making. Avoid similar fates by maintaining a comprehensive asset inventory and consulting professionals regularly. Doing so ensures your estate plan remains current, considers all potential tax liabilities, and reflects your evolving intentions. The right choices today can prevent heartache and loss tomorrow.

What Successful Estates Did Right

Consider a family that established a charitable giving strategy as part of their estate plan. By setting up a family foundation, they ensured their legacy continued supporting causes they cared about deeply. This approach provided tax benefits and allowed family members to participate in philanthropic decisions, fostering a sense of unity and purpose.

Another example involves a business owner who executed a seamless succession plan. They identified and trained the successor years in advance, ensuring a smooth transition without disrupting operations. Their foresight preserved the business's value and maintained employee confidence and morale.

These successes stemmed from clear communication and strategic planning. These families aligned their estate plans with their values and goals by openly discussing intentions and leveraging legal instruments like trusts and foundations. Trusts played a pivotal role in managing assets and minimizing taxes, while clear directives avoided misunderstandings. These strategies are adaptable to various situations. Tax-efficient gifting, for example, reduces liabilities and strengthens family bonds through shared decision-making. These positive outcomes inspire proactive planning. By taking deliberate actions today, you can build a legacy that endures, ensuring future generations benefit from your foresight and generosity.

Chapter Five

Keeping Your Estate Plan Current

I magine the excitement of welcoming a new grandchild into your family. The joy is palpable, and amidst the celebrations, a quiet but essential task requires your attention: updating your estate plan. This moment of happiness is also a reminder of the evolving nature of life and the need to ensure your estate plan reflects these changes. Estate planning is not a static process. It should evolve as your life's circumstances shift. Major life events are timely cues to revisit and revise your plans, ensuring your intentions are honored and your loved ones are protected.

When to Update Your Plan for Life Events and Estate Planning

Significant life events are critical milestones that necessitate a review of your estate plan. These events include marriage or divorce, the birth or adoption of a child or grandchild, and the death of a beneficiary or trustee. Each of these occurrences can profoundly impact your estate plan. For instance, marriage might prompt you to add your spouse as a beneficiary or joint owner of assets. Conversely, divorce often requires removing an ex-spouse from your plan to prevent unintended inheritance. The arrival of a child or grandchild means reassessing guardianship arrangements and potentially setting up trusts to secure their financial future. When a beneficiary or trustee passes away, it's crucial to designate new individuals to fill these roles, maintaining the continuity and effectiveness of your estate plan.

These life events can alter the distribution of your assets and the roles of those involved in your estate plan. A marriage might lead to changes in beneficiary designations, ensuring a provision for your new spouse. The birth of a child necessitates appointing a guardian, someone you trust to care for your child if you cannot. Similarly, the death of a trustee demands a reevaluation. It would be best if you appointed a new trustee to manage your assets, someone who understands your wishes and will act in the best interest of your beneficiaries. These changes ensure that your estate plan remains a true reflection of your current circumstances and intentions.

Proactively updating your estate plan is vital. Regularly scheduled reviews, perhaps every three years, help maintain alignment with your current wishes. Immediate updates following significant life changes prevent lapses that could lead to unintended consequences. For instance, failing to update a beneficiary designation could result in an ex-spouse receiving assets you intended for your children. By actively managing your estate plan, you safeguard your legacy and provide clarity for your loved ones.

Consider the case of a family who neglected to update their estate plan after the birth of a new grandchild. The outdated plan should have included this newest member, inadvertently excluding them from any inheritance. In another example, a trust did not reflect the family's recent adoption, causing legal complications and delays in asset distribution. These scenarios highlight the importance of timely updates, underscoring the peace of mind that comes with a plan that accurately represents your current reality. By keeping your estate plan current, you can rest assured that your loved ones will be cared for as you wish.

Estate Plan Review Checklist

To ensure your estate plan remains up to date, consider using this checklist:

- **Review Beneficiary Designations**: Confirm they reflect your wishes, including recent births, adoptions, or marriages.

- **Assess Guardianship Appointments**: Ensure appointed guardians align with your current preferences and any new family dynamics.

- **Update Trustee Assignments**: If necessary, appoint new trustees to manage your assets effectively.

- **Reflect on Asset Distribution**: Verify that the distribution of assets aligns with your desired legacy.

Engaging with this checklist regularly helps maintain an estate plan that adapts to your life's changes and secures your intentions for the future.

Understanding Variations and Updated Laws

The legal landscape profoundly influences estate planning, which varies significantly from state to state. Each state has laws governing probate processes, and these differences can dramatically affect the management of your estate after your passing. For instance, some states require a lengthy probate process that can delay the distribution of assets. In contrast, others have streamlined procedures that expedite this process.

Additionally, state-specific tax implications can impact your estate's value. States like Oregon and Massachusetts have their estate tax exemptions, which can affect the amount of taxation of your estate at the state level. Understanding these nuances is crucial, as they dictate the legal framework within which your estate plan operates. By understanding and navigating these laws, you can ensure your estate plan aligns with the legal requirements, empowering you to make informed decisions about your estate.

Local expertise becomes invaluable when navigating these complexities. Consulting with an estate attorney who is well-versed in state regulations ensures compliance and helps avoid potential pitfalls. These professionals can provide insights into the intricacies of state laws that might take time to become apparent to those unfamiliar with them. Staying informed about legal changes is equally important. Laws can change, impacting the management of estates.

By keeping abreast of these updates, you can ensure your estate plan remains effective and aligned with current regulations. An attorney can provide guidance on how these changes might affect your plan, offering strategies to adapt accordingly. With the support and guidance of these professionals, you can navigate the complexities of estate planning with confidence and peace of mind.

Relocation introduces another layer of complexity. Moving to a new state can render parts of your existing estate plan obsolete, necessitating updates to align with local laws. Wills and trusts may need revisions to comply with state-specific requirements. For example, the state laws governing the validity of a will or trust can differ, affecting the execution of the trust.

Power of attorney laws may also vary, requiring adjustments to ensure your designated agent has the authority to act on your behalf. These variations can significantly impact your estate plan's effectiveness, underscoring the importance of revisiting and revising documents when you relocate.

Numerous resources can help those seeking to stay informed and understand state-specific legal updates. State bar association websites often provide valuable information on recent changes in estate planning laws, offering guidance on compliance and best practices. Additionally, online legal resources and databases can serve as tools to research state laws and understand their implications for your estate plan. Utilizing these resources helps ensure that your estate plan remains current and effective, reflecting your wishes and the legal framework within which it operates.

The Role of Power of Attorney in Estate Planning

The concept of a Power of Attorney (POA) is a cornerstone in estate planning, providing a mechanism to appoint someone to manage your affairs in your stead. A POA is a legal document that grants authority to an appointed agent, allowing them to act on your behalf in financial or health-related matters. This delegation can be as broad or as limited as you choose, tailored to your needs and circumstances.

There are different types of POAs, each serving distinct functions. A durable POA remains effective if you become incapacitated, ensuring the handling of your financial matters without interruption. A financial POA explicitly allows the agent to manage your monetary affairs, from paying bills to overseeing investments and safeguarding your interests when you cannot do so yourself.

In estate planning, powers of attorney play a versatile role, offering peace of mind that your affairs are managed according to your preferences. For example, suppose you cannot manage your finances due to illness or travel. In that case, a financial POA ensures that bills are paid, accounts are monitored, and investments are managed according to your wishes.

Similarly, a POA can extend to healthcare decisions, permitting your agent to make medical choices on your behalf if you are incapacitated. This authority can be critical in emergencies, ensuring your medical preferences are respected and acted upon when you cannot communicate them yourself. By designating a trusted agent, you retain control over your life, even when you cannot directly participate in decision-making.

Establishing a power of attorney involves several essential steps, beginning with selecting a reliable and trustworthy agent. This individual should be someone who understands your values and priorities and can make decisions that align with your wishes. Once chosen, the next step is legal documentation, where the scope of the agent's authority is clearly defined. You must sign this legal document, often notarized, to be enforceable, adhering to state-specific requirements. Clear documentation ensures financial institutions and healthcare providers recognize the agent's authority, preventing potential disputes or challenges to their decisions.

Common misconceptions about powers of attorney can lead to misunderstandings regarding their function and limitations. It's crucial to recognize that a POA is invalid after the principal's death, meaning nobody can use it to manage an estate posthumously. Additionally, the POA strictly defines the scope of the document itself; the agent can only act within the parameters you set. Scope means that while a POA provides significant authority, it does not grant unrestricted power. The agent must act within the bounds of the authority you've outlined, safeguarding your interests and following your directions. Understanding these limitations helps prevent misuse and reinforces the importance of detailed, clear instructions in the POA document.

Healthcare Proxies Ensure Following Your Wishes

In estate planning, the healthcare proxy is crucial, ensuring your medical preferences are respected when you cannot advocate for yourself. This legal document allows you to designate a healthcare agent—someone you trust implicitly—to make medical decisions if you become incapacitated. The healthcare proxy bridges the gap between your medical wishes and the reality of your health situation, empowering your chosen agent to act in your best interest. By clearly defining this role, you ensure that your healthcare choices are honored, even in the most challenging circumstances. The designated agent becomes the voice of your healthcare directives, tasked with making decisions that align with your values.

Effective communication is paramount when establishing a healthcare proxy. It is vital to have candid conversations with your designated agent, discussing your healthcare preferences, values, and any advance directives or living wills you may have. These documents provide additional guidance, outlining specific medical treatments you wish to receive or refuse. Open dialogue with family members also helps prevent misunderstandings and ensures everyone is aware of your choices. Discussing your intentions equips your agent with the knowledge needed to make informed decisions, reducing the potential for family disputes and emotional stress during critical times.

Legal requirements for establishing a healthcare proxy vary by state, necessitating adherence to specific forms and procedures. Most states require the proxy to be documented on a standardized form, often necessitating the presence of witnesses or notarization to ensure its validity. These steps protect the document's integrity, allowing medical professionals and institutions to recognize it. Familiarizing yourself with state-specific requirements is crucial, as it guarantees that your proxy is legally sound and enforceable. Compliance with these legalities ensures that your healthcare agent can act without impediment, assuring the handling of your medical care according to your wishes.

Consider a case where a healthcare proxy effectively mediated a complex medical decision. An older woman had established a proxy with her daughter as the agent. When she suffered a severe stroke, the daughter, guided by prior discussions and the mother's living will, made critical decisions about treatment options. This proactive planning avoided family conflicts; everyone understood and respected the mother's choices. In another scenario, a healthcare proxy helped resolve a family dispute when siblings disagreed on their father's care. Armed with clear directives, the appointed agent navigated the situation, respecting the father's wishes and ultimately bringing the family together. These examples underscore the importance of a well-prepared healthcare proxy, highlighting its role in safeguarding your healthcare preferences and maintaining family harmony during difficult times.

Best Practices for Reviewing and Revising Your Estate Plan

Estate planning is not a one-time task but a continuous process that requires regular attention. Regular review intervals are vital to ensure your estate plan remains aligned with your current circumstances and wishes. Consider scheduling annual or biennial reviews. These periods allow you to catch any changes that may have occurred over the year, such as fluctuations in asset values or shifts in personal circumstances. Additionally, arranging meetings with an estate planner during these intervals provides expert insight and guidance, helping you adapt your plan to any new developments or legal changes.

Certain areas demand focused attention when reviewing your estate plan. Asset value or ownership changes can significantly impact your estate's distribution and tax implications. Updating your plan to reflect these changes is essential, as accounting for all assets is appropriately allocated. Similarly, remember to check beneficiary information regularly to reflect your current intentions accurately. Whether due to births, deaths, or changes in relationships, keeping beneficiary designations up to date prevents unintended distributions and potential conflicts among heirs.

Comprehensive revisions are necessary to address all aspects of your estate plan. Examine legal documents to ensure they reflect your current wishes and comply with any new laws or regulations. This check includes updating trust terms and conditions to align with your evolving goals and circumstances. Trusts are dynamic tools that can adapt to changes in family dynamics or financial situations. Still, they require regular attention and updates to function effectively.

Practical tools and tips can facilitate thorough evaluations to aid in this process. Utilizing checklists for estate plan evaluation helps you to examine every detail, covering everything from asset inventories to legal document compliance. Digital tools for document management offer a modern solution, allowing you to easily store, organize, and access your estate planning documents. These tools can streamline the review and revision process, making it more efficient and manageable.

As this chapter concludes, remember that an estate plan is a living document. Its strength lies in its ability to adapt and evolve with your life. Regular reviews and revisions ensure your plan truly reflects your wishes. By maintaining this proactive approach, you secure your legacy and provide clarity for your loved ones. As we move forward, consider how these practices integrate into the broader framework of your estate planning strategy, setting the stage for the next chapter's insights.

Chapter Six

Navigating Estate Planning Challenges

You're standing at the edge of a vast forest, each tree representing a decision about your future and picking which decision is how estate planning can feel—an intimidating landscape filled with choices that seem overwhelming. Procrastination often stems from the fear of confronting mortality and the perception that this process is too complex to tackle. Many people delay estate planning because they do not want to face the reality of their eventual passing. It's a discomforting thought, and it's easier to put off decisions that feel so final. The legal jargon and financial details can seem impossible, creating a barrier that keeps you from taking the first step.

However, there are significant advantages to beginning your estate planning journey early. The peace of mind of knowing your affairs are in order cannot be overstated. When you plan early, you gain control over the distribution of your assets, ensuring that your wishes are honored. This foresight provides security for you and your loved ones, as they won't be left navigating a complex legal system in an already difficult time. Early planning also allows for more flexibility in decision-making, allowing you to adjust your plan as life changes. By addressing estate planning now, you can avoid the rushed decisions often accompanying last-minute preparations.

To overcome procrastination:

- Start by setting small, achievable goals.

- Break down the process into manageable steps.

- List your assets, then consider who you want to inherit them.

- Set deadlines for each task, creating a timeline that guides you through the process without overwhelming you.

This method clarifies what you must do and provides a sense of accomplishment as you complete each step. Consider also creating a vision board where you map out your estate planning goals visually. Doing so can remind you daily what you want to achieve, motivating you to keep moving forward.

Success stories abound of individuals who have overcome their hesitation and taken control of their estate planning. Initially daunted by the perceived complexity, one couple decided to tackle their plan after learning about the peace of mind it could bring. They began by attending a seminar, which provided them with the knowledge and confidence to proceed. Their completed estate plan secured their assets and strengthened their relationship as they worked together to envision their future. Another individual shared how getting an early start on creating an estate plan allowed her to travel with the assurance that her affairs were in order, granting her freedom and peace.

Reflection Exercise

Set aside a quiet moment and reflect on what you want for your future and that of your loved ones. Consider your values and how they should show up in your estate plan. Write down your thoughts on what you hope to achieve through estate planning. This exercise can help clarify your goals and motivate you to begin the process with a clear vision.

Addressing the Common Fear of Mistakes and How to Fix Them

Estate planning often conjures a shadow of fear, primarily rooted in the prospect of making irrevocable mistakes. This fear is not unfounded; the legal complexities involved can seem daunting. Many worry about committing legal errors that might invalidate their plans or lead to unintended consequences. The anxiety of missing a crucial detail or misinterpreting legal jargon is a common barrier to moving forward. Concerns about family disputes also weigh heavily on one's mind. The thought of leaving behind a legacy that sparks conflict among loved ones is distressing. These fears, while understandable, should not paralyze progress.

Mistakes in estate planning are not as irreversible as they might seem. You can amend them with the correct guidance. Professional advice plays a vital role here, offering an expert eye to spot and rectify potential pitfalls. Estate attorneys and financial advisors can provide the reassurance needed to navigate this terrain. They offer tailored solutions, ensuring that your documents reflect your intentions accurately. When finding an error, amending estate planning documents is usually possible. The amendment might involve revising a will or updating trust terms to align with your goals. These professionals can also help anticipate changes in laws that may affect your plan, ensuring compliance and relevance.

Preventative measures can further mitigate the risk of mistakes. Implementing regular reviews and updates keeps your estate plan current and aligned with your evolving circumstances. This proactive approach helps catch discrepancies before they become issues. Clear communication with your advisors is also crucial. Openly discussing your goals and concerns allows them to tailor advice and strategies effectively. This transparency builds trust and ensures everyone is on the same page.

Consider the tale of a family who discovered a significant oversight in their will. The document, drafted years prior, no longer reflected their wishes due to changes in family dynamics. Upon realizing this, they consulted an estate attorney, who guided them through the amendment process. The will was revised to accommodate current circumstances, preventing future disputes and ensuring their intentions were honored.

Another example involves a trust dispute arising from ambiguous terms. The beneficiaries were at odds over interpretations, leading to tension and potential legal battles. They achieved clarity by engaging with a mediator, revisiting the trust's language, and resolving the dispute.

These examples underscore the importance of vigilance, communication, and professional support in maintaining an effective estate plan. Understanding that you can correct mistakes with the right approach alleviates fear and fosters confidence in managing your estate.

Where to Find Trustworthy Resources and Reliable Information

Finding reliable information can feel like navigating a dense fog when you embark on the estate planning path. The plethora of online resources can be both a blessing and a curse, providing abundant information and leaving you vulnerable to misinformation. The challenge lies in discerning which sources are credible.

Professional legal websites, recognized law firms, or estate planning associations offer a wealth of dependable information. These sites often publish articles and resources from experienced estate attorneys specializing in current laws and best practices.

Government publications are another cornerstone of reliability. They provide up-to-date legal guidelines and tax regulations pertinent to estate planning. Websites like the Internal Revenue Service (IRS) or your state's judicial branch can offer invaluable insights into the legal frameworks that govern estate planning.

Evaluating the reliability of online information is crucial to ensuring your decisions are informed and accurate. Begin by checking the credentials of the author or organization publishing the information. Look for qualifications, such as legal degrees or certifications, and a history of expertise in estate planning. Verifying information through multiple sources can also bolster its credibility. Cross-referencing facts with several reputable sites helps confirm accuracy and consistency. Beware of sites that make grand promises or offer overly simplistic solutions to complex problems, as these often need more depth and nuance. Instead, prioritize resources that present a balanced view, acknowledging potential challenges and offering pragmatic solutions.

In addition to online resources, traditional forms of information remain invaluable. Reputable books and publications can provide a solid foundation of knowledge. Estate planning guides written by legal experts delve into the nuances of estate management, offering detailed explanations and real-world examples. Financial planning magazines can also be a rich source of information, often featuring articles by seasoned financial advisors highlighting innovative strategies and market trends that may impact your estate plan. These publications usually come with a pedigree of editorial oversight, ensuring content is accurate and relevant.

Despite the wealth of information available, consulting with professionals remains a cornerstone of effective estate planning. Estate attorneys and financial advisors bring expertise that is difficult to match through independent research alone. They can offer personalized advice tailored to your unique circumstances, helping you navigate complex legal and financial landscapes.

Remember not to underestimate the value of a second opinion. Even if you feel confident in your knowledge, having a professional review of your plan can uncover potential oversights or areas for improvement. Their insights can provide clarity and peace of mind, ensuring your estate plan is robust and aligned with your goals.

DIY Estate Planning Risks and Rewards

The allure of do-it-yourself (DIY) estate planning lies in its promise of cost savings and personal control. Cutting out professional fees is especially appealing if you're working with a tight budget or your estate appears straightforward. It offers the chance to take charge, learn, and understand the intricacies of your own financial and legal landscape. Many find satisfaction in crafting a plan that feels intimately personal, tailored entirely by their hand. However, this approach has its pitfalls. The absence of legal expertise presents a significant risk.

Estate planning involves complex laws and regulations that vary by state and jurisdiction. With the guidance of a professional, you may overlook critical legal requirements, leading to documentation that needs to be completed or corrected. Such errors can invalidate your estate plan, leaving your assets unprotected and your intentions unmet. The consequences of these oversights often become apparent only when it's too late to amend them. For those considering a DIY approach, thorough research is a non-negotiable step.

Educate yourself on the specific laws and requirements that pertain to your situation. Utilize reputable templates and software designed to guide you through the process. These tools can provide a framework, but they should always retain the insight of a seasoned professional. It's also wise to have your DIY efforts reviewed by an attorney. This review helps catch potential mistakes and provides peace of mind, knowing that your plan meets legal standards. Consider the case of a couple who successfully crafted their estate plan. They began by conducting extensive research and using a high-quality software package to draft their documents.

After completing their plan, they consulted an estate attorney for a review. The attorney provided valuable feedback, helping them refine their strategy and address areas they had overlooked. This proactive approach resulted in a robust estate plan that reflected their wishes and protected their assets.

Contrast this with an individual who opted for a DIY will without seeking professional advice. Unfortunately, the document contained numerous errors and ambiguities. Upon her passing, these issues led to a prolonged probate process and disputes among her heirs. Being intended as a cost-saving measure resulted in significant legal fees and family discord.

These stories underscore the potential benefits and drawbacks of DIY estate planning. While it offers a degree of independence and cost-effectiveness, it demands a high level of diligence and an understanding of its limitations. The stakes are high, and the margin for error is small. For those who choose this path, the key lies in balancing personal initiative with professional insight, ensuring that your estate plan is legally sound and aligned with your intentions.

Family dynamics can pose significant challenges when it comes to estate planning. Differing expectations among heirs often lead to misunderstandings, especially when emotions run high. Each family member may have a unique perspective on what they believe they deserve, shaped by personal relationships and experiences. Sibling rivalries, too, can exacerbate these tensions, turning what should be a straightforward process into a battleground of disputes. These rivalries complicate the process by the inherent emotional weight of estate planning, where inheritance can become entangled with feelings of love, legacy, and loss. Acknowledging these complexities is the first step in addressing them effectively.

Open communication is crucial in navigating these turbulent waters. Families must strive for transparency when discussing estate plans. Family meetings can serve as a platform for airing concerns and aligning expectations. By involving all stakeholders, you ensure that everyone feels heard and valued. This inclusivity fosters trust and reduces the likelihood of surprises that could lead to conflicts later. During these discussions, it's essential to approach the conversation with empathy, recognizing each person's perspective and the emotions they bring to the table. This openness can mitigate misunderstandings and pave the way for a smoother estate planning process.

Conflict resolution strategies are essential tools in your estate planning toolkit. Mediation offers a neutral ground where a professional can guide the family through contentious issues, helping to find common ground without resorting to legal battles. Arbitration can also effectively resolve disputes, providing a binding decision that respects each party's concerns. Establishing clear terms and conditions within the estate plan can preempt conflicts by providing a structured framework for handling potential disagreements. These strategies empower families to address issues constructively, preserving relationships and ensuring the estate plan reflects the collective wishes of all involved.

Consider a family that faced an inheritance dispute after the passing of their patriarch. Tensions ran high, with siblings at odds over asset distribution. The family chose mediation, allowing a third party to facilitate dialogue and guide negotiations. Through this process, they reached an agreement that honored their father's wishes while respecting each sibling's concerns.

Another example involves a family trust agreement, where clear terms outline each beneficiary's responsibilities and entitlements. This clarity prevented disputes and ensured a smooth transition of assets.

These examples demonstrate the power of proactive communication and conflict resolution in estate planning. They highlight the importance of addressing family dynamics with care and foresight, ensuring that the estate plan serves its purpose without fracturing familial bonds. As we move forward, consider how these strategies can be applied to your situation, fostering an environment of understanding and cooperation.

Chapter Seven

Tax Implications and Financial Considerations

Y ou just inherited a beautiful family heirloom—a painting passed down through generations. Yet, with this treasure comes a hefty financial burden: taxes. Understanding estate and inheritance taxes is crucial, as these taxes can significantly impact what you leave behind. The government assesses estate tax on the transfer of the total value of your estate upon death. The federal government assesses this tax on the estate before distribution to beneficiaries, which can significantly reduce the estate's overall value. In contrast, the recipients are responsible for the inheritance tax of an estate. It's a tax on the portion of assets each beneficiary receives, varying by state and potentially affecting the net inheritance.

Understanding tax thresholds and exemptions can bring a sense of relief. The substantial federal estate tax exemption allows transferring estates worth up to a certain amount tax-free, shielding many estates from federal taxes. However, state-specific inheritance taxes can still apply, with each state setting its exemption limits. This understanding is essential to minimize the tax burden on your estate and ensure your beneficiaries receive their intended inheritance without unexpected deductions.

Anticipating and planning for potential tax liabilities can significantly reduce the net value of your beneficiaries' inheritance. This proactive approach can ensure your estate plan's intended impact, making it crucial to anticipate and plan for potential tax liabilities. Calculating estate tax liability involves assessing the total value of your estate and subtracting any applicable exemptions. The remaining amount is subject to tax rates, which can be steep. Similarly, determining inheritance tax depends on the beneficiary's relationship to the deceased and the amount they inherit. Different classes of beneficiaries may face varying tax rates, affecting how you allocate your estate.

Understanding complex tax laws can be a significant accomplishment. Misunderstandings about estate and inheritance taxes abound. Many mistakenly believe these taxes apply to all estates when only estates exceeding specific thresholds are affected. Furthermore, confusion often arises between state and federal tax laws, leading to miscalculations and unexpected liabilities. Clarifying these distinctions ensures your estate plan is tax-efficient and aligns with your goals. Consider an estate that surpasses the federal exemption limit, subjecting it to substantial taxes. Beneficiaries might also be liable for state inheritance taxes, depending on their relationship to the decedent and state-specific laws.

Charitable Trusts and Donations provide for a Tax-Advantaged Giving

Charitable trusts represent a powerful tool in estate planning, fulfilling philanthropic goals while providing tax benefits. A Charitable Remainder Trust (CRT) allows you to donate assets, such as cash or stocks, to an irrevocable trust. This trust generates income for you or non-charitable beneficiaries for a fixed period and donates the remaining assets to a chosen charity. This structure supports charitable causes, reduces taxable income, and offers a partial tax deduction. Similarly, Charitable Lead Trusts (CLTs) provide income to a charity for a set time before transferring the remaining assets to your beneficiaries, potentially reducing estate taxes. These trusts facilitate giving while ensuring your estate remains tax-efficient.

Charitable donations through estate planning yield significant tax advantages. When you make a charitable contribution, you can claim an income tax deduction, lowering your taxable income. Additionally, charitable bequests in your will or trust can reduce estate taxes by decreasing the taxable estate's value. This dual benefit allows you to support meaningful causes while safeguarding your financial legacy. Establishing a family foundation or using donor-advised funds offers further flexibility. These vehicles enable you to direct donations over time, allowing you to address emerging community needs or personal philanthropic interests.

Consider a family that established a charitable trust, providing income to support their lifestyle while ensuring the remaining assets benefit a local arts foundation. This thoughtful planning enriched their community and reduced their estate's tax burden. Similarly, a legacy gift, facilitated through a bypass trust, can have a lasting impact by funding scholarships or community programs. Another strategic way to manage charitable giving is through irrevocable life insurance trusts. Individuals set up these trusts to own a life insurance policy on your life. When you pass away, the policy pays proceeds to the trust, which then distributes the funds to your chosen beneficiaries and charitable organizations. This strategy ensures that policy proceeds benefit both heirs and philanthropic organizations and can reduce the size of your taxable estate.

Reducing Legal Fees and Achieving Cost-Efficiency in Estate Planning

Estate planning can be costly, with several factors contributing to the expenses. The complexity of estate documents often drives up costs. Drafting a comprehensive estate plan involves multiple legal documents, each tailored to specific needs and circumstances. These documents require careful attention to detail to ensure they align with your intentions and comply with legal standards. Additionally, the hourly rates of legal professionals add to the financial burden. Estate attorneys charge for their expertise, and the time spent drafting, revising, and consulting can quickly accumulate, especially if your estate plan is intricate. To manage these costs effectively, consider several strategies.

One such strategy is to opt for flat-fee estate planning services where possible. These services provide a set price for creating an estate plan, offering predictability and saving money compared to hourly billing. In this manner, you pay a fixed amount for the entire estate planning process, regardless of the time spent or the complexity of the plan.

Another approach is to prepare preliminary documents before meeting with an attorney. Organizing your financial records, listing assets, and outlining your goals can reduce the time needed for consultations. This preparation streamlines the process, allowing the attorney to focus on refining rather than gathering information. Technology plays a pivotal role in minimizing estate planning costs.

Online estate planning tools and software offer accessible alternatives to traditional methods. These platforms guide you through creating primary estate documents, reducing the need for extensive legal intervention. They provide templates, step-by-step guidance, and legal advice, which can significantly reduce the time and cost of hiring an attorney for every aspect of your estate plan.

Additionally, digital document management enhances efficiency, enabling easy sharing and storage of essential files. By leveraging these technological advancements, you can achieve a cost-effective estate planning process.

Consider a family using online tools to draft their estate plan, significantly reducing legal fees. They found the software user-friendly, providing templates and guidance that allowed them to complete most of the work independently. This approach freed up resources for more complex aspects of their estate, where professional advice was indispensable. In another scenario, a couple streamlined their estate planning by negotiating fees with their financial advisor. By discussing their budget upfront, they secured a fee structure that met their needs without compromising quality. Free community estate planning workshops also offer valuable insights and resources at no cost. These workshops provide an opportunity to learn from experts and connect with others navigating similar challenges. By exploring these strategies, you can craft an estate plan that balances thoroughness with financial prudence, preserving your assets for those who matter most.

Financial Implications and Benefits of Trusts vs. Wills

Choosing between a trust and a will can shape your estate's future. Trusts often entail higher initial costs than wills. They require legal expertise to set up, ensuring precise language and compliance with state laws. Maintenance of a trust involves periodic reviews and potential amendments, adding to its cost. However, this investment can yield significant savings by avoiding probate, a lengthy and expensive legal process required for wills. Probate can deplete estate value and delay asset distribution, which trusts sidestep entirely. Additionally, trusts offer privacy since their terms are not subject to public records, unlike wills.

The long-term benefits of trusts extend beyond immediate financial savings. Trusts provide ongoing asset management, allowing the trustee to make informed decisions about investments and distributions, even if you become incapacitated. This feature ensures your estate remains productive and aligned with your goals. Trusts also offer tax efficiencies through strategic asset allocation, potentially reducing the estate's tax burden. Asset protection is another crucial advantage, as specific trust structures shield assets from creditors and legal claims, preserving wealth for future generations. These benefits make trusts a compelling choice for those seeking comprehensive estate management.

When deciding between a trust and a will, consider the complexity of your estate and family needs. A trust's flexibility in managing these assets might be beneficial if your estate includes diverse assets, such as real estate and investments. Conversely, a will suffice if your estate is straightforward and primarily involves cash or personal property. Assess your distribution goals, including how and when beneficiaries receive their inheritance. Trusts allow staggered distributions based on age or milestones, often resulting in a lump-sum transfer. These considerations help align your estate plan with your personal and financial objectives.

Consider the scenario of a family using a trust to maintain financial control and flexibility. By transferring assets to a trust, they ensured that funds were available for a child's education, with the remaining assets distributed upon reaching adulthood. This arrangement provided peace of mind and financial security, adapting to the child's changing needs. In contrast, a will might offer straightforward asset distribution. For example, an elderly couple with a modest estate chose a will to simplify the transfer of their home and savings to their children. This decision minimized legal complexities and allowed for a direct inheritance, reflecting their desire for simplicity.

Economic Considerations for Future-Proofing Your Estate

In planning your estate, it is crucial to consider economic trends that could impact your asset values over time. Inflation, for instance, erodes purchasing power, meaning that the money you leave behind may stretch farther than you intended. As costs rise, the value of fixed-income investments might diminish, affecting your beneficiaries' financial stability. Keeping an eye on interest rates is equally important, as they influence the cost of borrowing and the returns on savings. Rising rates can offer better returns on savings. Still, they also increase the cost of debt management, which can impact overall estate value.

Planning for increased longevity and healthcare costs is another essential aspect. With people living longer, you must account for potential healthcare expenses in your retirement planning. Long-term care insurance is one option to mitigate these costs, offering coverage for extended care needs without depleting your estate. Estimating healthcare costs in retirement involves considering medical inflation and personal health history. Preparing for these expenses ensures your estate can support your lifestyle and care needs without compromising your financial legacy.

Global economic factors also play a significant role in estate planning. Currency fluctuations can affect international assets, altering their value and the estate's total worth. If you have investments or properties abroad, changes in exchange rates can impact their dollar value, influencing how you allocate your estate. Additionally, global market volatility requires a watchful eye on investment strategies. Economic shifts abroad can ripple through financial markets, affecting asset prices and returns. Ensuring your estate plan accounts for these variables helps maintain asset value across international boundaries.

Adaptive planning is crucial to accommodate economic shifts. Regularly reviewing investment strategies allows you to respond to market changes and align your portfolio with your goals. Flexibility in asset allocation decisions helps mitigate risks and capitalize on growth opportunities. Adapting your estate plan can preserve and enhance asset value as markets fluctuate. Regular updates ensure your estate remains robust and responsive to local and global economic landscapes.

Avoiding Common Pitfalls with Probate Costs

Navigating probate can be costly, with expenses arising from various sources. Executor fees are notable, as executors manage the estate's distribution and finances, often charging a percentage of the estate's value or an hourly rate. Appraisal fees also contribute significantly, as estate assets require valuation to determine their worth for distribution and tax purposes. These costs can quickly accumulate, reducing the estate's value and impacting the beneficiaries' inheritance. However, several strategies can help minimize these expenses, preserving more of your estate's value for your heirs.

Streamlining the probate process is one such approach. Organizing your estate documents and providing clear instructions for executors can reduce the time and complexity involved, lowering costs. Utilizing small estate affidavits can also be effective for estates under a certain value threshold, allowing for a simplified probate process that bypasses some of the traditional steps. Planning plays a crucial role in reducing probate costs. Proper titling of assets and adding a joint owner or transfer-on-death designation can prevent these assets from going through probate altogether.

Establishing joint ownership where appropriate ensures that assets pass directly to the co-owner upon death, avoiding probate. Consider the example of an estate that effectively avoided probate through a living trust.

The family ensured a seamless transfer without court intervention by placing assets in a trust. In another scenario, a family agreement waived executor fees, further reducing costs and preserving the estate's value. These cases illustrate the effectiveness of proactive planning in managing probate expenses.

Leveraging Trusts for Maximum Tax Efficiency

Trusts offer a strategic avenue for optimizing tax outcomes, and choosing the proper structure is crucial. Grantor Retained Annuity Trusts (GRATs) allow you to transfer assets while retaining an annuity for a set period. The remainder passes to beneficiaries, potentially free of gift tax, making GRATs attractive for appreciating assets. Dynasty trusts, designed for multigenerational planning, permit wealth to be preserved and grown, bypassing estate taxes for future generations. These trusts leverage the generation-skipping transfer tax exemption, shielding assets from repeated taxation as they pass from generation to generation.

Irrevocable trusts play a pivotal role in tax planning, effectively removing assets from your estate. By placing assets in an irrevocable trust, you diminish the taxable estate's value, thus reducing estate taxes. This structure also protects assets from creditors and legal claims, safeguarding wealth for heirs. When properly structured, these trusts control asset distribution while providing substantial tax savings. Evaluating your tax goals and family dynamics is essential when selecting the appropriate trust. Consider how much control you wish to retain versus the potential tax benefits. Balancing flexibility and tax savings requires thoughtful consideration of your estate's complexity and long-term objectives.

Consider families employing charitable lead trusts to support philanthropic goals while achieving tax efficiency. These trusts allocate income to charities for a specified term, reducing the taxable estate's size. Upon conclusion, the remaining assets revert to family beneficiaries, minimizing estate taxes. Similarly, special needs trusts offer a dual benefit, providing for a dependent's care while preserving eligibility for government assistance. Tailoring these examples illustrates how trusts can meet diverse needs, optimizing tax outcomes while securing financial futures.

The Essential Documents Every Estate Plan Needs

Building a solid estate plan is like constructing a house; each document is a critical component supporting the structure. At the foundation lies the last will, which dictates the distribution of your assets after your passing. It names your beneficiaries and appoints an executor to manage your estate's affairs, carrying out your wishes accurately. Alongside it, a living will and advance directives operate differently, focusing on your medical preferences. These documents guide healthcare providers on your treatment choices, reflecting your desires when you cannot communicate them yourself.

Trust agreements are another pillar, offering a mechanism to manage and protect your assets during and after your lifetime. They detail the terms that hold and distribute your assets, providing flexibility and control over your estate's management. Beneficiary designations, often overlooked, are equally vital. They specify who should receive assets from accounts like life insurance policies and retirement funds, aligning with your overall estate intentions. These documents must coordinate seamlessly; for instance, a will should complement a living trust, ensuring no contradictions that could lead to legal disputes.

Precision and clarity are paramount to drafting these documents effectively. Working with legal professionals enhances accuracy, reducing the risk of errors. It's crucial to use clear, specific language that leaves no room for misinterpretation. Common pitfalls include overlapping provisions that conflict with each other or failing to update documents after life changes, such as marriage or the birth of a child. Regular reviews and updates are necessary to align your estate plan with current circumstances, protect your legacy, and honor your intentions.

What Is a Power of Attorney and Why You Need It

A power of attorney is a vital tool in estate planning, providing a legal framework for delegating decision-making authority. It allows you to appoint someone you trust to handle your financial and healthcare affairs if you cannot do so. This instrument ensures continuity in managing your life's affairs, preventing disruption during periods of incapacity. There are different types of powers of attorney, each serving distinct purposes. A general power of attorney grants broad authority to your agent, enabling them to manage various aspects of your financial life. In contrast, a durable power of attorney remains effective even if you become incapacitated, ensuring your agent can continue making decisions on your behalf.

Understanding the scope of power of attorney is crucial. Limited powers of attorney restrict the agent to specific tasks or timeframes, offering flexibility for particular needs. Doing so can be beneficial for managing a one-time financial transaction or specific healthcare decisions. Conversely, general powers provide more comprehensive authority, allowing your agent to manage various financial and medical matters. Selecting a trusted agent is a critical decision. It would help to choose someone trustworthy, reliable, and who shares your values. This person must act in your best interests, aligning with your goals and preferences. Consider their ability to handle financial responsibilities and willingness to make tough healthcare decisions.

Imagine a scenario where you are bedridden due to a medical condition. With a power of attorney, your appointed agent can manage your finances, pay bills, and monitor investments. Similarly, you face a healthcare crisis and need help communicating your wishes. Your agent can make informed medical decisions that reflect your values. This legal arrangement provides peace of mind, knowing that your affairs are in capable hands and protected during challenging times.

Prepare for the Unexpected with Healthcare Directives

Healthcare directives are vital documents that ensure your medical care aligns with your preferences when you cannot voice them yourself. These directives include advanced healthcare directives and living wills, articulating your treatment preferences. By specifying the medical interventions, you want or wish to avoid, you provide clarity and direction to healthcare providers. This foresight is crucial, as it guides decisions about life-sustaining treatments, pain management, and end-of-life care. Expressing these preferences beforehand alleviates the burden on loved ones, who might otherwise face difficult choices during emotionally charged times.

An effective healthcare directive comprises several vital elements. It should outline specific treatment preferences, detailing your desires regarding resuscitation, artificial nutrition, and other critical interventions. These preferences must be clear and precise to ensure they are honored. Additionally, appointing a healthcare proxy or agent is essential. Where a designated individual acts as your advocate, making medical decisions per your outlined wishes. Selecting a proxy who understands your values and is willing to advocate on your behalf is an essential step in the directive process.

Drafting and communicating your healthcare directives require careful consideration. Working with healthcare professionals during drafting can help ensure your instructions are medically sound and feasible. Once completed, share these directives with your family and medical team.

Making multiple copies accessible to those who need them can prevent misunderstandings and follow your wishes. Real-life scenarios highlight the importance of these directives. In critical care situations, healthcare providers rely on your directives to make immediate decisions, ensuring interventions align with your values. Likewise, during end-of-life care, these documents provide a roadmap for treatment, allowing you to maintain control over your medical journey.

Best Practices for Keeping Your Documents Updated

In the realm of estate planning, the only constant is change. Personal circumstances evolve, the government amends laws, and what once seemed sufficient can quickly become outdated. Regularly reviewing your estate planning documents is not just advisable; ensuring your intentions remain clear and enforceable is necessary. Life changes such as marriage, divorce, the birth of a child, or the acquisition of new assets can significantly impact your estate plan. These events necessitate updates to reflect your current wishes and safeguard against unintended consequences. Moreover, staying abreast of updates in laws and regulations is crucial. Legal shifts can render aspects of your estate plan obsolete or non-compliant, potentially leading to disputes or financial penalties.

A structured review approach can be invaluable in maintaining an effective estate plan. Consider conducting a thorough review of your documents after any significant life event. Additionally, scheduling annual or biennial reviews ensures your strategy aligns with your evolving goals and circumstances. This proactive approach helps catch discrepancies or outdated provisions before they become problematic. When making amendments, it's essential to work with legal professionals to ensure all changes are legally binding. A simple oversight can lead to complexities and challenges, undermining your estate plan's effectiveness.

Neglecting updates can lead to significant consequences. Outdated estate documents often result in conflicts among heirs, as unclear intentions or overlooked changes can cause disputes. Legal challenges are another risk, potentially invalidating your carefully crafted plans. For instance, an outdated will might not account for newly acquired assets, leading to unintended beneficiaries and family discord. These scenarios underscore the importance of keeping your estate plan current, protecting your legacy, and ensuring your wishes are honored.

Chapter Eight

Real-Life Applications and Case Studies

A family is gathered around a living room, each member representing a unique piece of their shared history and future. In blended families, where stepchildren and biological children coexist, estate planning becomes a delicate balancing act. The challenges are numerous, with each family member bringing their perspectives and needs to the table. In these situations, ensuring everyone feels valued and fairly treated requires more than good intentions; it demands strategic planning and open communication.

One such scenario involves a couple with children from previous marriages. Here, the goal is to balance the interests of all children, providing for each without igniting conflict. Attaining this goal can be particularly challenging when family members have different expectations or past relationships influence current dynamics. One practical approach is to establish separate trusts for each child. This approach ensures that assets are distributed according to specific needs and circumstances, eliminating ambiguity. By doing so, the couple can provide for their children in a way that aligns with their goals and wishes. Additionally, life insurance policies can help equalize inheritances, ensuring that each child receives a fair share, regardless of the value of other assets.

Communication is vital in these complex family arrangements. Regular family meetings offer a platform for discussing estate intentions, allowing everyone to voice their concerns and understand the reasoning behind decisions. Documenting these discussions within the estate plan further clarifies intentions, reducing the risk of disputes. In one case, a family successfully navigated these complexities by engaging in open dialogues facilitated by an experienced estate planner. With their expertise in estate planning and interpersonal skills, this professional guided the family through difficult conversations, ensuring all voices participated and the plan reflected collective values.

Lessons from such cases highlight the importance of flexibility and adaptability in estate planning. As family dynamics evolve, so too should the estate plan. Evolution requires ongoing communication and a willingness to adjust strategies as needed. An experienced estate planner can offer invaluable guidance, helping identify potential issues such as changes in family structure or financial circumstances and propose solutions that accommodate these circumstances. They create a plan and ensure it remains relevant and effective over time.

Unique Considerations for Business Owners and Estate Planning

Consider the inspiring scenario of a business owner who has spent decades building a company from the ground up. As retirement approaches, the challenge of succession planning looms large. Without a clear plan, the future of the business is uncertain, and the owner's legacy is at risk. The owner faces the intricate task of ensuring the continuity of business operations while protecting assets from personal liabilities. In such cases, establishing a clear succession plan becomes crucial. This plan outlines who will take over leadership roles and how ownership will transition, ensuring the business thrives beyond the owner's tenure.

Trusts play a significant role in facilitating a seamless transition of business ownership. Creating a family business trust allows the owner to place company shares into a trust managed by a trustee according to specified terms. This structure keeps the transition private by avoiding probate. It provides clear instructions for the trustee, minimizing disputes among family members or business partners. Additionally, using buy-sell agreements to manage changes in ownership provides a predetermined path for buying out a departing owner's shares. These agreements offer security and clarity, reducing uncertainty during transitions.

The tax implications of transferring business assets are another layer of complexity. Utilizing estate tax exemptions can help minimize the tax burden on the estate, preserving more of the business's value for heirs. For closely held businesses, leveraging valuation discounts can further reduce taxable estate value, providing financial relief to the beneficiaries. These strategies require careful planning and a thorough understanding of tax laws to ensure compliance and optimization.

Insights from this case study emphasize the importance of involving business partners in the planning process. Their input and cooperation are beneficial and essential to crafting a plan that reflects the business's needs and vision. Regularly updating business valuations and succession plans ensures the strategy remains relevant and practical. As the industry evolves, so should the estate plan, adapting to new challenges and opportunities to protect the owner's legacy and the company's future.

Addressing Trusts for the Special Needs of those requiring Dependent Care

Imagine a family navigating the complexities of estate planning with a dependent who has special needs. This scenario demands careful planning beyond the traditional approach to ensure long-term financial security without jeopardizing the dependent's eligibility for government benefits. Special needs trusts offer a tailored solution, allowing families to provide supplemental support without affecting benefits like Medicaid or Supplemental Security Income (SSI). Families craft these trusts to address specific care requirements, catering to the unique needs of the dependent. The distinction between first-party and third-party special needs trusts is crucial. A first-party trust, funded by the dependent's assets, may require Medicaid reimbursement upon the beneficiary's death. In contrast, a third-party trust, supported by family or friends, does not carry such requirements, offering more flexibility in asset distribution.

The success of a special needs trust hinges on the choice of trustee. Selecting someone with experience in special needs planning is paramount. This trustee must understand the intricacies of benefit regulations and the care requirements of the beneficiary. Establishing a care committee can also provide oversight and support, ensuring the trust operates smoothly and aligns with the beneficiary's evolving needs. In one case, a family chose a professional fiduciary as trustee, alongside family members forming a care committee. This setup provided expertise and personal insight, balancing professional management with familial support.

Key takeaways from such cases emphasize the need for regular reviews and updates to the trust. As care needs change, the trust should adapt, ensuring continuous support. Legal guidance is indispensable in navigating benefit regulations and avoiding pitfalls that could disrupt eligibility. Families must stay informed about legislative changes, maintaining compliance and maximizing the trust's effectiveness. The journey of planning for a dependent with special needs is complex but manageable. It requires careful planning, informed decision-making, and ongoing commitment to the dependent's well-being.

Real Estate and Multiple Properties in Estate Planning

Imagine the intricate web of managing multiple real estate holdings, each property with its own set of challenges and opportunities. Consider a family owning several rental properties and a cherished vacation home by the coast. The complexities of maintaining these assets can be immense, from the daily management of tenants to the seasonal upkeep of a second home. Such properties' Estate planning must account for operational responsibilities and the long-term vision for asset transfer. Inheritance and tax considerations become pivotal as the family seeks to preserve these properties for future generations. This consideration involves understanding the current value of each property and projecting the potential tax liabilities that may arise upon transfer.

Strategic estate planning methods are essential for addressing these complexities. One practical approach is establishing real estate limited liability companies (LLCs) for liability protection.

By placing properties under the ownership of an LLC, the family can shield their assets from potential lawsuits or claims related to the properties. This structure also simplifies the process of transferring ownership, as shares of the LLC can be distributed rather than the properties themselves. Using qualified personal residence trusts (QPRTs) can benefit primary residences. QPRTs allow homeowners to transfer their home to a trust while retaining the right to live there for a specified term, effectively removing the property from the taxable estate and minimizing estate taxes.

Transferring real estate involves significant tax implications that require careful navigation. Understanding capital gains tax is crucial, as property selling can trigger substantial tax liabilities. However, some strategies leveraging tax-deferred exchanges allow property owners to defer capital gains taxes by reinvesting the proceeds into a similar property. This strategy can preserve the estate's value by minimizing immediate tax burdens. Accurate property appraisals are vital in correctly assessing the estate's value and meeting tax obligations.

Lessons from this case study highlight the importance of thorough appraisals and considering family dynamics in property distribution decisions. Accurate appraisals reflect the estate's actual value, preventing disputes among heirs. Understanding family preferences and relationships can guide equitable distribution, aligning the estate plan with the family's collective goals.

Planning to Protect Your Online Digital Assets

In today's digital age, the scope of your estate extends beyond physical assets. Digital assets now form a crucial part of modern estate planning. These include your social media accounts, online banking profiles, investment accounts, and digital media collections such as photos and music. Each element holds financial and sentimental value, and their management requires careful consideration. Social media accounts, for example, store memories and represent personal and sometimes professional identities. Securing and appropriately distributing online banking and investment accounts that contain financial resources are essential. Meanwhile, digital media collections capture moments and creative works you may wish to pass on to loved ones.

Managing digital assets after death presents unique challenges. Accessing these assets can become a significant hurdle due to password protection and stringent security measures. Many people must keep a comprehensive record of their access credentials, leaving executors needing help to retrieve important information. Additionally, terms of service agreements from digital platforms often restrict access to accounts by anyone other than the original owner, complicating the transfer process. These issues can lead to losing or locking assets indefinitely, depriving beneficiaries of their intended inheritance.

Organizing and protecting your digital assets should be a priority in addressing these challenges. Start by creating a detailed inventory that lists all digital accounts and their respective usernames and passwords. This inventory is a roadmap for your digital executor, guiding them through accessing and managing your online presence. Using password managers can significantly assist in securely storing and updating access credentials, ensuring they remain accessible to trusted individuals without compromising security.

Including digital assets in your estate planning documents is crucial. Explicitly stating your wishes regarding digital asset management in your will or trust helps clarify your intentions. Appoint a digital executor, someone specifically tasked with handling your digital affairs and managing these assets according to your directives. This executor will navigate the complexities of digital platforms, adhering to your outlined preferences and ensuring that your online legacy is preserved and transferred as you intended. This approach secures your digital assets and provides peace of mind, knowing that your physical and digital estate is accounted for and protected.

Lessons from Real Life in Overcoming Common Challenges

Estate planning often presents unexpected hurdles, mainly involving multiple stakeholders with varied expectations. A common challenge is managing family disputes over asset distribution. Imagine a scenario where siblings contest each other's shares, leading to strained relationships. Such conflicts can arise from perceived inequities or misunderstood intentions, often fueled by emotional grievances. Another challenge is handling complex financial portfolios, where the sheer volume of assets and their diverse nature can overwhelm even the most organized individuals. These situations require careful navigation and a strategic approach to ensure a fair resolution.

Anticipating potential issues is critical to preempting these challenges. One effective strategy is directly incorporating conflict resolution mechanisms into the estate plan. These may include arbitration clauses or appointing a neutral third party to mediate disputes, providing a structured process for addressing disagreements. Regularly updating the estate plan to reflect current circumstances further prevents conflicts, ensuring the plan remains relevant and aligned with the family's evolving needs. Blending open lines of communication and keeping beneficiaries informed can minimize misunderstandings, fostering a more harmonious environment.

Consider the example of a family that successfully mediated a discussion to reach a consensus on asset distribution. By facilitating an open dialogue, they identified each member's concerns. They worked collaboratively to address them, resulting in a mutually agreeable solution. In another instance, a family utilized professional mediators to resolve disputes, allowing for an impartial perspective that guided negotiations and ultimately led to a satisfactory outcome for all parties involved. These cases underscore the value of proactive measures and professional assistance in navigating complex estate planning situations.

Ensuring clear documentation and communication throughout estate planning is crucial for readers. Articulating intentions and outlining roles within the plan can prevent ambiguity and reduce the likelihood of disputes. Seeking expert advice, especially for complex financial matters, can provide clarity and guidance, ensuring the plan is comprehensive and practical. Recognizing and addressing potential challenges head-on equips you to manage your estate confidently, safeguard your legacy, and foster family unity.

Understanding Community Property vs. Common Law States

Understanding the differences between community property and standard law states is crucial for effective asset management in estate planning. Community property states, including regions like California and Texas, treat most assets acquired during marriage as jointly owned by spouses. Community property means these assets are typically divided equally between the partners upon divorce or death. In contrast, standard law states like New York and Florida operate on a title-based system. Here, ownership is determined by whose name appears on the title or deed, meaning that assets acquired by one spouse remain solely theirs unless otherwise specified.

The distinction between these systems significantly impacts estate tax liability and asset distribution. In community property states, the equal division of assets can simplify tax obligations, as both spouses are equally responsible for the estate. Conversely, the individual ownership model can lead to more complex tax scenarios in standard law states, especially if one spouse holds significantly more assets. Thus, understanding which system applies is vital for planning effective tax strategies and ensuring your estate plan aligns with the legal framework of your state.

Tailor-made planning strategies are necessary to navigate these differences. In community property states, structuring property agreements can clarify asset division and protect individual interests. This agreement might involve prenups or postnups specifying the handling of assets. In standard law states, trusts can be a powerful asset management tool. For example, a revocable trust can hold assets in a way that ensures they are distributed according to your wishes, bypassing the title-based system.

Consider a scenario where a couple in a common-law state chooses to create joint tenancy arrangements. This agreement ensures that upon the death of one spouse, the surviving partner automatically inherits the property, avoiding probate. Meanwhile, establishing a revocable trust in a community property state can manage the property while alive and define its distribution after death, providing both control and clarity. Understanding these systems and implementing appropriate strategies is essential for protecting your assets and ensuring your estate plan functions as intended. Recognizing the nuances of your state's property laws safeguards your interests and provides peace of mind when managing your estate.

Chapter Nine

Choosing and Working with Professionals

Like standing at the foot of a mountain, your estate plan is ready to climb. But you are unsure of the best route. The path ahead is steep and filled with obstacles with high stakes. This challenge is how estate planning can feel, especially when complexities arise. Engaging the right professionals—lawyers and financial advisors—can be akin to having experienced guides. They bring clarity and direction, helping you confidently navigate the intricacies of estate planning.

Understanding when to enlist professional help is crucial. Complex family dynamics often necessitate mediation by someone with expertise. Imagine a scenario where family members have competing interests. Without a neutral party to mediate, these situations can quickly become contentious. A lawyer experienced in estate planning can mediate, facilitate discussions, and include all voices. They provide a framework for resolving disputes amicably, preserving family harmony while safeguarding the integrity of your estate plan.

In cases involving high-value estates, the stakes are even higher. Such estates often have significant tax implications, such as [specific examples of tax implications]. These require sophisticated strategies to minimize liabilities. A financial advisor with in-depth knowledge of tax laws can offer invaluable insight. They work to structure your estate in a way that optimizes tax efficiency, preserving your wealth for future generations. Their role extends beyond mere advice; they actively manage investments and trusts, aligning them with your goals and the latest legal requirements.

Business ownership introduces another layer of complexity. Succession planning is a critical component of estate planning for business owners. As you plan for the future, consider how your business will transition to the next generation or a new owner. A professional advisor can help you develop a comprehensive succession plan, addressing potential challenges and ensuring a smooth transition. This planning protects not only the business's financial health but also its legacy. Advisors can help balance personal and business assets, ensuring neither is compromised. Their expertise in both financial and legal aspects is indispensable, offering a holistic approach that covers all bases.

Evaluating the need for professional help involves assessing your personal and financial situation's complexity. Start by considering the intricacies of your family dynamics and the potential for conflict. Are there multiple stakeholders with differing interests? Next, examine the size and scope of your assets. High-value estates, international assets, or business ownership significantly increase complexity. If you find yourself overwhelmed by the legal and financial intricacies, it's time to seek professional guidance. Comfort with managing these aspects on your own is a good indicator of when to engage an expert. Suppose you feel uncertain or need more expertise. In that case, professional assistance can bridge that gap, providing peace of mind and executing your estate plan flawlessly.

Consider scenarios where professional guidance proves advantageous. For estates with international assets, navigating the differing legal systems and tax implications can be daunting. A professional with experience in international estate planning can streamline the process, ensuring compliance with all relevant laws. Similarly, families with special needs dependents face unique challenges. Crafting a plan that addresses both immediate and future care requires specialized knowledge. An advisor can guide you in establishing trusts and other mechanisms to provide long-term financial support without jeopardizing eligibility for government benefits. These examples demonstrate professionals' value, transforming complex challenges into manageable tasks and providing relief and reassurance.

Recognizing the expertise and experience professionals offer in estate planning is essential. They possess in-depth knowledge of state and federal laws, ensuring compliance and preventing costly mistakes. Their strategies for minimizing taxes and legal fees can lead to significant savings. You can lay a solid foundation for your estate plan by engaging professionals early in planning. This proactive approach provides clarity and peace of mind, knowing that your plan is in capable hands. The collaboration with skilled advisors transforms estate planning from a daunting task into a streamlined process, empowering you to take control of your future.

Reflection Exercise

Take a moment to assess your estate planning needs. Consider the complexity of your family dynamics and the value of your estate. Are there business interests or international assets involved? Write down your thoughts and identify areas where you feel uncertain. This reflection can help clarify whether professional assistance would be beneficial. Use this exercise as a starting point to engage with advisors, ensuring that your estate plan is comprehensive and aligned with your goals.

When and How to Seek Legal Assistance Help

Estate planning involves complex legal considerations, where the stakes and risks of errors are high. Legal assistance is indispensable in navigating these intricacies. A well-versed estate planning attorney ensures that your plans comply with current laws, avoiding costly legal pitfalls. These professionals understand the nuances of estate law, which vary from one jurisdiction to another. They offer guidance aligning with state and federal regulations, providing peace of mind that your estate plan is legally sound. Their expertise extends to drafting documents that withstand scrutiny, safeguarding your intentions. Legally sound documents protect your estate from challenges, ensuring your wishes are honored without unnecessary disputes. By engaging an attorney, you access this specialized knowledge, reducing the risk of errors that could compromise your estate.

Certain situations necessitate seeking legal help, mainly when complexities arise. Professional mediation is essential if your estate involves intricate family dynamics—such as blended families or disputes among heirs. An attorney can help navigate these delicate situations, crafting a plan that addresses each party's concerns while protecting your interests. Similarly, significant asset portfolios require sophisticated strategies to manage and distribute wealth effectively. An estate planning lawyer can guide you in structuring your assets to maximize benefits and minimize taxes. Their insight into asset protection and distribution ensures that your estate remains intact, providing for your beneficiaries as intended. Legal assistance is also crucial when your estate involves unique assets, such as intellectual property or international holdings, with specific legal considerations.

Choosing the right legal professional involves careful evaluation. Consider their experience and specialization in estate planning. A qualified attorney should have a proven track record in handling similar cases, demonstrating expertise in the specific areas your estate requires. Seek recommendations from trusted sources, such as friends or financial advisors, and review client testimonials to gauge satisfaction with their services. Online reviews and legal directories can provide additional insights into their reputation and capabilities. Evaluate their approach to client relationships, ensuring they prioritize your needs and communicate effectively. A lawyer who listens and understands your goals will be better equipped to translate them into a robust estate plan.

Working effectively with legal professionals involves preparation and communication. Before meeting with your attorney, organize your documents and outline your questions. A clear understanding of your assets, liabilities, and objectives will facilitate productive discussions, allowing the attorney to provide targeted advice. This preparation saves time and addresses all critical issues. Maintain open communication channels with your lawyer, regularly updating them on any changes in your circumstances that may affect your estate plan. Transparency fosters trust and enables the attorney to adjust your plans as needed. Schedule periodic reviews to assess the plan's alignment with your evolving goals and legal requirements.

Estate Planning Document Checklist

Consider creating a checklist of necessary estate planning documents for your attorney meetings. Include items such as the last will, trusts, property deeds, and lists of assets and liabilities. This checklist ensures you have readily available pertinent information, streamlining the process and facilitating thorough legal analysis. By preparing these documents in advance, you maximize the efficiency of your consultations, enabling your attorney to focus on crafting a comprehensive plan tailored to your needs.

Engaging a legal professional is not merely about compliance but crafting a plan that reflects your values and provides for your loved ones. An estate planning attorney is your advocate, translating your wishes into legally binding documents that stand the test of time. Their role preserves your legacy and respects your intentions. With their guidance, you confidently navigate the complexities of estate planning, securing the future for yourself and your beneficiaries.

Key Questions to Ask When Evaluating Potential Advisors

When considering advisors for your estate planning, the vetting process is crucial. You need professionals who understand the intricacies of estate planning and align with your personal and financial goals. Start by asking about their experience in estate planning. Interviewing them ensures they know what is necessary to handle complex situations that might arise. An advisor with a solid track record will have encountered various scenarios, from navigating tax implications to managing diverse family dynamics. Experience strongly indicates an advisor's ability to provide sound guidance. Moreover, inquire about specific cases they have handled that resemble your circumstances. Their past work offers insight into their real-world application of knowledge and problem-solving skills.

References and client testimonials are invaluable. They offer a window into the advisor's past performance and client satisfaction. When speaking with references, ask about the advisor's strengths and areas for improvement. Did they meet expectations? Were they proactive in addressing concerns? These insights help you gauge whether the advisor can meet your needs.

Additionally, client testimonials can reveal the advisor's reputation within the community. An advisor with positive reviews is more likely to be trustworthy and reliable. Don't hesitate to reach out to other clients for their firsthand experiences. Their feedback can provide reassurance about the advisor's capabilities and professionalism.

Discuss fee structures and billing practices upfront. Understanding how an advisor charges for their services is essential to avoid unexpected expenses. Some advisors charge flat fees, while others bill hourly or take a percentage of assets under management. Clarify which method they use and how it aligns with your budget. Knowing their fee structure helps you evaluate the cost-benefit ratio of their services. It also ensures transparency, preventing any hidden fees from arising later. Discussing billing practices also opens the door to negotiations, allowing you to reach an agreement that suits both parties. This conversation is crucial to avoid misunderstandings and maintain a healthy working relationship.

Compatibility and trust form the backbone of a successful advisor-client relationship. Assessing communication style and responsiveness is critical. You want an advisor who listens to your concerns and communicates clearly, providing timely updates and advice. Their ability to explain complex concepts understandably is vital. A good advisor should use language that resonates with you, avoiding jargon that might confuse or alienate you. Evaluate their responsiveness to your inquiries; an advisor who promptly addresses your questions is more likely to be attentive and engaged. This engagement fosters trust, ensuring you're comfortable sharing personal and financial information essential for effective planning.

Evaluating shared values and understanding client goals is another cornerstone of the advisor-client relationship. Your advisor should appreciate your vision for your estate and offer strategies that align with your objectives. Knowing your vision requires understanding your values, whether they involve preserving family wealth, supporting charitable causes, or ensuring equitable distribution among heirs. An advisor who shares your values will likely provide recommendations that reflect your priorities. They should also respect your decisions, offering guidance without imposing their views. This alignment ensures that your estate plan reflects your true intentions, making you confident in the advisor's recommendations.

Conducting thorough background checks on potential advisors is a step you must pay attention to. Check their professional licensing and certifications to ensure they are qualified to provide estate planning advice. Licensing signifies adherence to industry standards, while certifications demonstrate a commitment to ongoing education and expertise. Review disciplinary records or complaints to identify past issues that might raise concerns. This information is often available through professional regulatory bodies or industry associations. A clean record indicates a high level of professionalism and ethical conduct. Additionally, consider their involvement in professional organizations, as active participation often reflects a dedication to their field.

Initial consultations play a crucial role in the evaluation process. They offer an opportunity to gauge the advisor's approach and determine if it matches your needs. Prepare questions and topics for discussion in advance. This preparation allows you to assess the advisor's knowledge and problem-solving abilities. During the meeting, observe how the advisor addresses your concerns and offers solutions. Their ability to listen and provide clear, thoughtful responses is a good indicator of their competence. Please pay attention to their demeanor and professionalism, as these qualities will influence your comfort level when working with them. A successful initial consultation makes you confident in the advisor's capabilities and eager to progress.

As you finalize your choice of advisors, remember that they become integral partners in your estate planning process. They advise and work alongside you, translating your goals into actionable strategies. You build your estate plan on a solid foundation by evaluating their experience, compatibility, and trustworthiness. This collaboration empowers you to make informed decisions, safeguarding your legacy and respecting your wishes. With the right advisors, you can easily navigate the complexities of estate planning, setting the stage for a secure and prosperous future.

Chapter Ten

Overcoming Common Objections and Misconceptions

E nvision you are sitting with a cup of coffee, looking over your financial papers. You've heard about living trusts but are still determining if they suit you. You may have thought living trusts are too complex, costly, or only valid for the wealthy. These misconceptions are familiar, yet they often prevent individuals from making informed decisions about their estate planning. Let's unravel these myths and explore the accessible truth about living trusts.

One widespread belief is that living trusts are exclusively for the affluent. This myth persists because trusts are often associated with large estates and high-net-worth individuals. However, the truth is quite different. Living trusts offer benefits that apply to estates of all sizes. They provide a structured way to manage and distribute assets, regardless of the estate's value. Whether you own a modest home or more significant assets, a living trust can streamline the process and offer peace of mind. It's an inclusive tool designed to protect assets and ensure your wishes are honored, regardless of your financial standing.

Another misconception is that living trusts eliminate all estate taxes. While they offer some tax advantages, they are not a catch-all solution for tax liabilities. The primary benefit of a living trust is probate avoidance, which can save time and money. However, estate taxes depend on various factors, such as the total value of your estate and applicable federal or state laws. A living trust helps organize your estate and can be part of a broader tax strategy. Still, it's essential to consult tax professionals to understand its limitations. You can craft a comprehensive plan addressing your tax concerns by doing so.

Many also assume that setting up a living trust is simple and inexpensive. While establishing a trust may require an initial investment, it is often cost-effective. The expenses related to probate, such as court fees and legal expenses, can quickly surpass the costs of creating a trust. Moreover, trusts offer flexibility in managing and distributing assets, allowing you to adjust as needed. This adaptability is invaluable, particularly when faced with changing family dynamics or financial circumstances. Setting up a trust is straightforward with the proper guidance, making it accessible to many.

Consider a family that has successfully bypassed the probate process by establishing a living trust. They avoided the lengthy and public probate proceedings, allowing their assets to be distributed efficiently and privately to beneficiaries. Doing so saved money and preserved family harmony, as the trust clearly outlined the distribution plan. Similarly, individuals have found that living trusts provide flexibility in asset management. By retaining control over their trust, they could adjust beneficiaries and terms as their circumstances changed, offering a tailored approach to their evolving needs.

Reflective Exercise

As you consider your estate planning options, consider your financial goals and family dynamics. Consider the assets you wish to protect and how a living trust might fit into your strategy. Write down any questions or concerns, and seek professional advice to explore how a living trust could meet your needs. This reflection can clarify your objectives and guide you in making informed decisions about your estate plan.

Understanding the practical benefits of living trusts is crucial. They offer privacy, avoiding the public disclosure of your estate details during probate. This privacy can be particularly appealing if you value confidentiality in financial matters. Additionally, bypassing probate ensures a timely transfer of assets, reducing potential delays that could impact beneficiaries. By structuring your estate through a living trust, you gain control and flexibility that traditional wills may lack. This control allows you to navigate life's uncertainties with a plan that adapts to your needs, preserving your legacy as you intend.

Overcoming Procrastination and Why Now Is the Time

Picture this: you're sitting on your couch, flicking through channels or scrolling through your phone, and the thought of estate planning crosses your mind. You might quickly brush it aside, convincing yourself there's plenty of time to deal with it later. This mindset is common but can lead to significant issues down the line. When you delay estate planning, you risk increased legal fees and complications. The longer you wait, the more complex your financial situation might become, and legal costs inevitably rise with that complexity. Unintended asset distribution is another consequence of procrastination. Without a clear plan, your assets may not go to the people or causes you care about, leaving loved ones to navigate a potentially contentious and confusing process.

One of the biggest hurdles in initiating estate planning is the psychological barrier many face. The idea of confronting one's mortality is daunting and can create an emotional block. It's not easy to think about life after you're gone, yet it's a conversation most of us need to have. Then, there's the perceived complexity of the process. Legal jargon, numerous documents, and the fear of making mistakes can seem overwhelming. This perception often leads to avoidance, as the task feels insurmountable. However, recognizing these barriers is the first step toward overcoming them. Understand that feeling overwhelmed is natural, but it shouldn't prevent you from taking action.

To combat procrastination and move forward with your estate planning:

- Start by setting small, achievable goals.

- Break the process into manageable steps.

- Instead of tackling everything individually, focus on one aspect at a time.

- Consider listing your assets or deciding who you want as your executor.

Completing these tasks one by one builds momentum and confidence. Creating a timeline for completion can also be beneficial. Set realistic deadlines for each task and hold yourself accountable. This structured approach transforms a daunting task into a series of more minor, more approachable actions.

Real-life examples can serve as powerful motivators. Take the story of a family who began planning early. They settled an estate without disputes or legal battles simply because they had a clear plan. Their proactive approach saved them from potential financial strain and preserved family harmony. Contrast this with another family who delayed planning. They faced unexpected legal fees and a prolonged probate process, which strained family relationships and caused unnecessary stress. These stories illustrate the tangible benefits of early planning and demonstrate how taking action sooner rather than later can safeguard your loved ones' futures.

Reflect on your situation and consider the impact that procrastination could have. Think about the people you care about and how you want your assets to support them. This reflection can act as a catalyst, encouraging you to prioritize estate planning. Once you take the first step, each subsequent step becomes more accessible. Remember, the ultimate goal is to ensure your wishes are honored, and those you care about are protected. By addressing estate planning now, you position yourself to make informed decisions that can benefit you and your family.

Why Estate Planning Is Important for Everyone and Isn't Just for the Wealthy

Many believe the estate planning process is a privilege reserved for the wealthy. This belief overlooks the universal benefits of estate planning, regardless of one's financial status. At its core, estate planning is about organizing your affairs to ensure your loved ones are cared for, and your wishes are honored. It provides a roadmap for the distribution of your assets, preventing potential disputes and unnecessary legal battles. By planning your estate, you can offer clarity and direction to your family, ensuring a smooth transition during what could otherwise be a tumultuous time.

Consider a young couple with children. They may not have vast wealth, but they have something invaluable—the responsibility of securing their children's future. Without a clear estate plan, questions arise about who will care for the children if the parents can no longer do so. By designating guardians through a will, these parents can ensure that their children are cared for by trusted individuals, aligning with their values and wishes. Knowing that someone you trust will look after your children brings immeasurable peace of mind, highlighting one of the many non-financial benefits of estate planning.

For individuals with modest savings or assets, estate planning remains crucial. It distributes even small assets according to your wishes rather than left to the state's default rules. This planning can prevent your belongings from becoming entangled in legal disputes, which can be costly and time-consuming. By clearly outlining your intentions, you reduce the likelihood of misunderstandings and conflict among your heirs, preserving family harmony and creating a legacy that reflects your values and priorities.

Estate planning extends beyond wealth management. It encompasses decisions about healthcare and end-of-life wishes. By including directives such as a living will or medical power of attorney, you ensure that your healthcare preferences are respected, even if you cannot communicate them yourself. This aspect of planning relieves your family from making difficult decisions during emotional times, providing them with guidance and confidence in fulfilling your wishes. Additionally, estate planning can help maintain family harmony by reducing potential conflicts over healthcare decisions, which can strain relationships.

The stories of individuals from diverse backgrounds highlight the broad applicability of estate planning. Consider the individual who meticulously documented their preferences for treatment, ensuring they planned for healthcare decisions. This foresight allowed their loved ones to act confidently and by their wishes without second-guessing or conflict. Couples with modest estates often find immense peace of mind through estate planning. By clearly outlining their intentions, they protect their assets, however modest, from becoming a source of discord among family members. These testimonials illustrate that estate planning is not about the size of your estate but the clarity and security it provides to those you care about.

In summary, estate planning is vital for anyone who wishes to protect their loved ones and distribute their assets according to their wishes. It is not a process reserved for the affluent but a practical necessity for everyone, regardless of financial standing. By planning your estate, you provide a gift to your loved ones—a clear and concise plan that honors your intentions and alleviates potential burdens. As we move forward, let us explore the next steps in safeguarding our futures.

Chapter Eleven

Leveraging Technology in Estate Planning

Y ou're at home, enjoying coffee while your tablet illuminates the room. With just a few taps, you can access your estate planning documents. This once-distant dream is a reality, thanks to the innovative digital tools available in estate planning. These tools empower you to easily manage, update, and secure your estate plan, seamlessly integrating into your daily life. As technology advances, the convenience and necessity of integrating digital solutions into estate planning become more apparent, putting you in control of your legacy.

An Overview of Digital Estate Planning Tools

In the realm of digital estate planning, several essential tools stand out. Online platforms for drafting wills and trusts provide a foundation for your estate plan. These platforms offer templates that simplify creating essential documents like revocable trusts and powers of attorney. By guiding you through each step, they reduce intimidation and make the process more accessible. Digital vaults, another cornerstone, act as secure storage for your estate documents. They keep everything organized and easily accessible, ensuring your loved ones can find what they need when the time comes. These digital vaults often include features for uploading and managing various documents, from insurance policies to birth certificates, ensuring comprehensive coverage of your estate.

The benefits of these digital tools are numerous. They offer unparalleled ease of access, allowing you to manage your estate plan from virtually anywhere with an internet connection. This accessibility lets you update your documents in real time, ensuring they always reflect your current wishes and circumstances.

Time-saving features streamline the process, reducing the need for multiple in-person consultations and lengthy paperwork. Many tools also provide automated alerts for document reviews, prompting you to revisit your plan periodically and make necessary updates. This functionality ensures your estate plan remains relevant and effective over time, adapting to life's changes.

Despite their advantages, digital tools have limitations, with security being a primary concern. Storing sensitive information online presents risks of data breaches and unauthorized access. Therefore, choosing platforms with robust security measures, such as encryption and two-factor authentication, is crucial to protect your data. Additionally, while generic templates provide a good starting point, they may need more customization for complex estate plans. Unique family dynamics or specific asset types may require tailored solutions that digital platforms alone cannot fully address. Consulting with a professional to complement digital efforts is advisable for such cases.

Digital Tool Selection Checklist

When selecting a digital estate planning tool, consider the following checklist to ensure it meets your needs:

- **Security Features**: Look for encryption, two-factor authentication, and regular security audits.

- **Customization Options**: Ensure the platform allows modifications to suit your specific circumstances.

- **User Interface**: Evaluate the ease of use and accessibility from multiple devices.

- **Customer Support**: Check for available support to assist with any technical issues.

- **Integration Capabilities**: Confirm the tool can incorporate various document types and formats.

These considerations will guide you in choosing a tool that enhances your estate planning process and aligns with your security and customization needs, providing peace of mind as you manage your legacy.

Utilizing Checklists and Worksheets for Effective Planning

Imagine estate planning as a complex puzzle. Each piece, from assets to beneficiaries, must fit perfectly. Checklists and worksheets act as your blueprint, guiding you through each step and noticing everything. These tools provide structured guidance, breaking down the process into manageable tasks. This structure helps reduce the risk of oversight and errors, making the planning process more manageable. Following a checklist, you can systematically account for every detail, from documenting assets to designing beneficiaries. Conversely, worksheets serve as interactive templates that allow you to organize information succinctly and clearly.

Consider an asset inventory checklist. This tool prompts you to list all your belongings, from real estate to digital assets. It ensures you get all critical components, aiding in a more comprehensive estate plan. Another example is a beneficiary designation worksheet, which helps clarify who will inherit specific assets. This worksheet encourages you to think carefully about your choices and document your wishes. Additionally, a healthcare directive preparation list can guide you in outlining your preferences for medical treatment, providing peace of mind by respecting your desires in times of need. These examples demonstrate how checklists and worksheets cover essential aspects of estate planning, helping to simplify and streamline the process.

One cannot overstate the flexibility of customizing worksheets to fit personal needs. Every estate is unique, and your planning tools should reflect this individuality. By modifying templates, you can address specific family dynamics or include unique asset categories that standard forms might overlook. For instance, if you have a collection of rare art, your asset inventory should account for these items separately. Customization allows you to adapt the planning process to your circumstances, ensuring a more effective and personalized estate plan. This adaptability is invaluable, particularly for families with intricate structures or unconventional assets, making you feel accommodated and understood.

Integrating checklists into your estate planning routine is straightforward yet powerful. Set reminders for periodic updates, ensuring your plan remains current as life changes. Regularly reviewing these documents keeps your plan relevant and reflective of your intentions. Digital versions offer easy access and modification, allowing you to update information promptly. This integration ensures that your estate plan evolves with you, adapting to new circumstances and maintaining its effectiveness over time. Incorporating these tools into your routine creates a dynamic estate plan to protect your legacy.

Apps and Software to Simplify Estate Management

In today's digital age, apps and software have revolutionized estate management, making it more accessible and efficient. Personal finance apps, for instance, provide robust tools for tracking assets, ensuring you always have a clear picture of your financial landscape. These apps allow you to monitor investments, check real-time balances, and even forecast future financial scenarios, offering a comprehensive view of your estate's health. Document management software, on the other hand, organizes and stores critical documents securely. These platforms ensure that everything from wills to insurance policies is cataloged and easily retrievable, simplifying updates and reviews. With these tools, managing your estate becomes less of a burden and more of an ongoing, manageable task.

These tools integrate seamlessly with your financial accounts, pulling data directly to provide an accurate overview of your estate's status. This integration ensures that all information is up-to-date, reducing the risk of oversight or error. Automated alerts play a crucial role here. They remind you of upcoming deadlines, like when to review your estate plan or update beneficiary information, ensuring nothing falls through the cracks. These alerts can be customized to fit your schedule, allowing for proactive estate management. Moreover, these apps often provide detailed analytics, offering insights into spending patterns, asset growth, and potential areas for improvement, aiding in more informed decision-making.

User experience is a critical factor in the effectiveness of these apps. Most come with user-friendly interfaces designed to be intuitive. This ease of use means you don't have to be technologically savvy to benefit from them. Many apps are optimized for mobile devices, allowing you to manage your estate on the go. This mobile accessibility ensures that you can make updates, check information, and stay informed, no matter where you are. Such features are particularly beneficial for busy people, providing flexibility and convenience. Additionally, many platforms offer personalization options, allowing you to tailor the dashboard to highlight the most relevant information for your situation.

Finding Credible and Up-to-Date Information using Online Resources

Navigating the digital landscape for estate planning information can feel overwhelming, with countless websites vying for attention. To ensure you're accessing reliable resources, start with government websites. They offer a wealth of legal guidelines and are updated regularly to reflect recent changes. Sites like the Internal Revenue Service (IRS) provide essential tax information that can impact your estate planning decisions. Another valuable resource is the American Bar Association's website, which offers insights into estate law and best practices. These authoritative and trustworthy platforms make them a solid starting point for any estate planning inquiry.

When evaluating the credibility of online information, it's crucial to assess the author's expertise. Look for credentials that indicate a background in law or estate planning. Cross-referencing information with multiple sources can further enhance reliability. For instance, if several respected sites provide the same guidance, it's more likely to be accurate. Be cautious of websites that lack transparency about their authors or sources. These sites may offer outdated or incorrect advice, potentially leading to costly mistakes in your estate planning. Always prioritize well-established platforms with a history of providing accurate and up-to-date information.

Staying informed about the latest legal changes is vital in estate planning. Laws and regulations can shift, impacting your estate plan's structure. Keeping abreast of these changes ensures your plan remains compliant and effective. Recent tax law updates, for example, can alter estate tax obligations, affecting asset distribution. Regularly checking trusted resources helps you adapt your plan to current legal standards. This vigilance protects your assets and ensures your estate plan aligns with your goals. Ignorance of legal changes can lead to complications, emphasizing the importance of using current information.

Consider bookmarking a few key sites for a list of trusted online resources. The IRS website offers comprehensive tax guidance, which is vital for understanding potential liabilities. The American Bar Association provides legal insights and educational materials on estate planning. These sites, along with government portals, are invaluable for staying informed. They offer a foundation of credible information, supporting your efforts to create a robust estate plan. Utilizing these resources enhances your understanding and ensures your estate plan reflects your wishes and the latest legal standards.

Protecting Your Digital Assets with Cybersecurity in Estate Planning

In the digital era, the security of your estate planning documents is paramount. Imagine the ramifications of identity theft, where stolen personal information is misused, leading to devastating financial and emotional consequences. Data breaches, the unauthorized access and retrieval of sensitive information, pose a significant threat to the integrity of your estate plan. Such intrusions can expose your assets to fraud, manipulation, and theft. The digital landscape, while offering convenience, requires vigilant protection measures to safeguard your legacy from these perils.

To fortify your digital assets, employ solid and unique passwords for all accounts related to your estate plan. A robust password should combine uppercase and lowercase letters, numbers, and symbols, making it difficult for hackers to decipher. Additionally, implementing two-factor authentication adds an extra layer of security. This method requires a second verification form, such as a code sent to your mobile device, before granting access. By doing so, even if a password is compromised, your accounts remain protected. Regularly updating your security measures is crucial as cyber threats evolve rapidly. Stay informed about the latest cybersecurity strategies to ensure your estate remains secure.

Legal and privacy considerations are integral to protecting digital estate assets. Including digital asset clauses in your will or trust documents is essential, specifying how these assets should be managed and by whom. Specifying the handling of these assets ensures clarity and direction for your executor or trustee, reducing potential disputes. Compliance with data protection laws, such as the General Data Protection Regulation (GDPR) or local equivalents, is also vital. These regulations govern handling personal data and protect against unauthorized use, providing a legal framework for safeguarding digital information.

Imagine a family discovering that inadequate cybersecurity measures compromised their loved one's estate documents. The breach delays the probate process and leads to financial loss as criminals exploit sensitive information. In contrast, imagine a case study where comprehensive digital asset protection was in place. This family utilized advanced security protocols and included digital instructions in their estate plan, ensuring a smooth transfer of information and assets free from cyber threats. These examples underscore the importance of robust cybersecurity measures and legal precautions in maintaining the integrity and security of your estate plan.

Using Virtual Consultations to Remotely Work with Professionals

Recently, virtual consultations have transformed how individuals engage with estate planning professionals. The convenience of remote meetings has become a significant advantage, allowing you to connect with attorneys and financial advisors without the constraints of geographical boundaries. This shift means you no longer need to travel long distances for in-person consultations, saving time and money. Virtual consultations often prove more cost-effective, as they reduce overhead costs associated with traditional office visits, potentially lowering service fees.

Virtual consultations typically involve videoconferencing tools, facilitating face-to-face communication with professionals. These platforms let you discuss your estate planning needs in real-time, ensuring clarity and understanding. Additionally, secure document-sharing platforms allow you to send and receive sensitive documents, such as wills and trusts, without compromising confidentiality. These tools provide a seamless experience, integrating various aspects of estate planning into one cohesive process. By leveraging technology, you can efficiently manage your estate from the comfort of your home.

The benefits of virtual consultations are numerous. You gain access to a broader range of expertise, not limited to local professionals. This expanded access allows you to seek specialists who can address specific needs, such as complex tax strategies or unique asset management. However, remote consultations also present challenges, including potential technical difficulties. More internet connections or unfamiliarity with digital tools can help communication. It's crucial to ensure your technology is up-to-date and reliable to maximize the effectiveness of these meetings.

Preparation is critical to conducting an effective virtual consultation. Before your meeting, organize all necessary documents and information. This organization ensures that the consultation is focused and productive. Verify that your internet connection is stable to avoid disruptions. Additionally, familiarize yourself with the video conferencing platform to ensure a smooth experience. By taking these steps, you can make the most of your virtual consultations, ensuring your estate plan is comprehensive and well-managed.

Chapter Twelve

Learning from Experts and Real-World Experiences

I magine the reassurance of sitting down at a table with a diverse group of professionals, each an expert in a different aspect of estate planning. This chapter invites you into those conversations, offering insights and guidance from attorneys, tax advisors, and financial planners. These are the voices of experience, bringing clarity to the complex world of estate planning. Estate attorneys, for instance, are pivotal in shaping a comprehensive estate plan. They provide legal frameworks that ensure your wishes are legally binding and efficiently executed. They provide invaluable knowledge of probate laws and tax implications, ensuring your estate is managed according to your intentions and giving you peace of mind.

Certified financial planners complement this expertise by focusing on your financial landscape. They help align your estate plan with your long-term financial goals, ensuring your assets are protected and positioned for growth. Their insights into investment strategies and risk management are crucial, particularly when navigating the intricacies of estate taxes. Together, these professionals create a robust support system, each contributing their unique expertise to craft a cohesive plan that safeguards your legacy.

You'll discover the importance of regular estate plan updates from these experts. Life is unpredictable, and as circumstances change, so should your estate plan. Whether it's a new addition to the family, a change in financial status, or a shift in your priorities, your estate plan must reflect these changes to remain effective. Please update your plan to avoid unintended consequences, such as outdated beneficiary designations or overlooked assets. By staying proactive and revisiting your estate plan regularly, you ensure it continues serving your best interests, giving you a sense of control over your future.

Emerging trends in estate planning, such as digital advancements, significantly shape modern strategies. Digital advancements have revolutionized how we manage and protect our assets. From online platforms that simplify document creation to secure digital vaults for storing essential documents, technology offers unprecedented convenience and security. Experts emphasize incorporating these tools into your estate plan, allowing seamless updates and real-time access to your records. This modernization not only streamlines the planning process but also enhances the accessibility and security of your estate. Understanding and adopting these trends can significantly improve the efficiency and effectiveness of your estate plan.

Throughout these interviews, specific themes emerge repeatedly. Experts highlight the common challenges individuals face embarking on their estate planning journey. A frequent issue is the misconception that estate planning is only necessary for the wealthy. In reality, everyone can benefit from having a plan in place, regardless of the size of their estate. Another challenge is the fear of making mistakes, often leading to procrastination. Experts advise breaking the process into manageable steps and seeking professional guidance to navigate complex decisions.

Expert Interview Highlights

Consider the highlights from these expert interviews to bring these insights to life. Many estate attorneys emphasize the significance of understanding who inherits assets upon your death and how to protect them from nursing home costs. Financial planner insights focus on minimizing estate taxes and leveraging digital tools for efficient asset management. Reflect on these takeaways and consider how they apply to your situation. What steps can you take to incorporate these expert strategies into your estate plan? By engaging with these insights, you empower yourself to make informed decisions that protect your legacy and provide peace of mind for your loved ones.

Real-Life Success Stories of Others' Experiences

Consider the story of a young family eager to secure their children's future in an uncertain world. They understood that an estate plan was about wealth, protection, and peace of mind. They defined their goals to ensure their children's well-being and educational opportunities. Communication played a pivotal role in their planning process. The couple engaged in open discussions with each other and their extended family, addressing potential guardianship and distribution concerns. This transparent dialogue minimized misunderstandings and fostered a cohesive approach to their estate. Central to their strategy was the effective use of trusts and wills. By establishing a trust, they ensured that their children would have access to financial resources for college and other life milestones, free from the complexities of probate. The will outlined their wishes, providing clarity and direction for their family. This careful planning safeguarded their children's future and reinforced family bonds.

Meanwhile, the experience of business owners who successfully navigated succession planning offers valuable lessons. These entrepreneurs recognized the importance of early preparation, understanding that transitioning a business requires time and thoughtful strategy. They began by identifying potential successors and involved them in critical decisions early on. This involvement fostered a sense of ownership and prepared successors for their future roles. A well-structured trust was instrumental in their planning, outlining the terms of business transfer and providing a clear roadmap for all parties involved. This legal framework ensured the business remained operational and prosperous throughout the transition. The success of this plan hinged on meticulous preparation and the ability to adapt to changing circumstances. By tailoring the plan to their specific needs and maintaining open lines of communication, the business owners ensured a smooth and successful transfer of leadership.

From these stories, several critical lessons emerge. Early planning and open communication are paramount. By addressing potential issues upfront, you can prevent conflicts and ensure your estate plan reflects your true intentions. Tailoring your plan to meet your family's or business's unique needs is equally important. Each situation is different, and a one-size-fits-all approach rarely works. Instead, customize your plan to accommodate specific circumstances, whether that involves setting up a trust for education or outlining a business succession strategy. Reflect on your situation and consider how these strategies might apply. Identify your personal estate planning goals and evaluate your current plan. Does it meet your needs and those of your loved ones? Are there areas that require adjustment or further discussion? Taking the time to reflect and plan can make a significant difference in the security and clarity of your estate.

Lessons Learned from Estate Planning Mistakes

In estate planning, the devil is often in the details. A frequently overlooked mistake is failing to update beneficiary designations. Life is dynamic, and as people marry, divorce, or welcome new family members, their estate plans must reflect these changes. Refrain from updating these designations to avoid unintended consequences, such as assets passing to an ex-spouse or bypassing a new grandchild. It's a simple oversight with potentially profound repercussions, disrupting the harmony of your intended estate distribution. By being aware of these pitfalls and avoiding them, you can feel at ease and prepared for the future.

Another common pitfall is the oversight of digital assets. As our lives become increasingly digital, so do our estates. Digital assets encompass everything from online bank accounts and digital currencies to social media profiles and personal blogs. It would be best to account for these in your estate plan to avoid complications. Executors may struggle to locate or access these assets, leading to prolonged probate processes and potential financial loss. Including digital assets in your estate plan ensures they are managed and transferred according to your wishes, preventing unnecessary stress for your loved ones.

The consequences of these mistakes can be severe. Consider the prolonged probate processes that can arise from an outdated will. Without clear directives, families may find themselves entangled in legal disputes, each party interpreting the deceased's intentions differently. These differences delay the distribution of assets and can strain familial relationships. Similarly, unintended asset distribution can occur when beneficiary designations are outdated. Assets might end up with individuals who the deceased no longer wished to benefit, causing potential discord among heirs.

Regular estate plan reviews are crucial to avoid these pitfalls. Setting a routine for reviewing and updating your estate plan ensures it remains aligned with your current life circumstances and intentions. This proactive approach helps catch changes in beneficiary status or the accumulation of new assets, digital or otherwise. A comprehensive asset inventory is another preventive measure. Maintaining a detailed list of all assets, including digital ones, takes notice of everything when planning your estate. This inventory should be revisited regularly, especially after significant life changes.

Real-life examples underscore the importance of vigilance in estate planning. Take the case of an outdated will causing family disputes. In this scenario, a father left a will that hadn't been updated in years, leaving his estate to a deceased sibling. The lack of clarity led to a bitter legal battle among his children, each with differing interpretations of his wishes. Another example involves unaccounted digital assets, complicating the estate settlement. The deceased had substantial cryptocurrency holdings but left no instructions or access details. Executors faced a daunting task, leading to delays and potential financial losses for the beneficiaries. These lessons highlight the importance of keeping your estate plan current and comprehensive, preserving your legacy as you intended.

Building a Network for Estate Planning with Community Support

Think of yourself as walking into a room filled with people who, like you, are navigating the complexities of estate planning. Here, you find a sense of camaraderie and shared purpose. Building a supportive community can transform the often daunting task of estate planning into a collaborative effort. Sharing experiences and advice with others who have faced similar challenges provides practical insights and emotional reassurance. This exchange of ideas allows you to gain diverse perspectives, offering solutions you might have yet to consider independently. It's a reminder that while estate planning is personal, you don't have to tackle it alone. You can learn from their successes and setbacks by connecting with others and adapting their strategies to fit your unique circumstances.

Support networks, both online and offline, offer a wealth of resources for those seeking guidance in estate planning. Online forums dedicated to estate planning provide a platform for you to ask questions, share experiences, and gain insights from others who have faced similar situations. These digital communities can be precious for accessing advice from a wide range of people, including those with diverse backgrounds and experiences. Local workshops, often hosted by community centers or financial institutions, offer another avenue for support. These gatherings provide educational opportunities and facilitate connections with professionals who can offer personalized advice. Engaging with these networks can help you stay informed about the latest trends and best practices in estate planning, ensuring your plan remains current and effective.

Collaborative planning with family and trusted advisors can further enhance your estate planning efforts. Joint decision-making processes allow for open discussion and factor in all voices. This approach can be particularly beneficial when involving multiple generations in planning. By including your children or other heirs in these discussions, you can educate them about the importance of estate planning and prepare them for future responsibilities. This collaborative effort fosters a sense of ownership and responsibility, encouraging all involved to contribute to the plan's success. It also allows you to address any potential concerns or conflicts before they arise, ensuring a smoother transition of assets and responsibilities.

Building and nurturing a network for estate planning support requires proactive engagement. Start by contacting community groups focused on estate planning or financial literacy. These groups often host events and workshops where you can meet others in similar situations. Leveraging social media can also effectively connect with like-minded individuals and join discussions on relevant topics. Platforms like LinkedIn or Facebook have groups dedicated to estate planning, where members share articles, resources, and personal experiences. By actively participating in these communities, you can stay informed, gain new perspectives, and build a support network that enhances your estate planning efforts.

When and How to Seek Help from Financial Advisors

When navigating the complexities of estate planning, financial advisors are crucial in guiding you through the maze of financial decisions. Their expertise extends beyond mere number-crunching. They offer a holistic approach to managing your estate, ensuring that every facet aligns with your financial goals. A financial advisor's primary function is comprehensive financial planning. This planning involves assessing your financial situation, projecting future needs, and crafting strategies to meet those objectives. By understanding your unique circumstances, they tailor plans that protect your assets and enhance your growth potential. Investment strategy development is integral to this process. Advisors analyze market trends and risk factors to recommend investment portfolios that align with your risk tolerance and financial ambitions. This strategic approach ensures that your estate plan is robust and resilient, capable of weathering economic fluctuations.

Knowing when to seek the assistance of a financial advisor can make a significant difference in the effectiveness of your estate plan. Major life changes or transitions, such as marriage, divorce, or the birth of a child, are pivotal moments that may necessitate a reevaluation of your financial strategy. These events often shift priorities and financial responsibilities, requiring expert guidance. Additionally, you possess a complex financial portfolio with various properties, investments, or business interests. In that case, the insight of a skilled advisor becomes invaluable. Their ability to synthesize diverse financial elements into a cohesive plan can prevent costly oversights and manage your estate efficiently.

Selecting the right financial advisor is a decision that warrants careful consideration. Begin by evaluating their credentials and certifications. Look for advisors with designations such as Certified Financial Planner (CFP) or Chartered Financial Consultant (ChFC), which indicate a high level of expertise and adherence to ethical standards. Experience with estate planning is equally important. An advisor well-versed in estate matters will better understand the nuances of managing and protecting your assets. They can provide insights into tax implications, legacy planning, and the integration of financial strategies with legal documents. A proven track record in estate planning equips the advisor to handle the complexities of your specific situation.

Working effectively with a financial advisor requires clear communication and a collaborative mindset. Begin by setting clear financial goals that define your estate planning objectives. Whether it's ensuring a comfortable retirement, funding your children's education, or leaving a charitable legacy, articulating these goals provides a roadmap for your advisor to follow. Regular review meetings are essential to keep your plan on track. These meetings offer an opportunity to assess progress, make adjustments, and address any concerns that may arise. Establishing a schedule for these reviews ensures that your estate plan remains dynamic and responsive to changes in your life and the economic landscape. By fostering a strong working relationship with your financial advisor, you empower yourself to make informed decisions, safeguarding your financial future and legacy.

Chapter Thirteen

Sustaining Your Legacy

Y ou can feel the warmth of sitting around a table with your family, sharing stories and laughter. You realize that these moments, though intangible, are vital parts of the legacy you will leave behind. While estate planning often brings to mind wills, trusts, and financial strategies, a legacy encompasses much more than material wealth. It includes the values you cherish, the traditions you uphold, and the memories you create with loved ones. These non-financial aspects of your legacy are as vital as any financial plan, providing a deep emotional connection and a sense of belonging for future generations.

Legacy planning involves more than passing down assets. It's about documenting family history and preserving the unique tales that define your lineage. Often told during gatherings, these stories can connect generations and instill a deep sense of identity and pride. Consider creating a family book or recording oral histories. These projects ensure that your descendants understand their roots and the journey that shaped your family. Likewise, passing down family recipes and traditions sustains cultural practices that might otherwise fade with time. These invaluable heritage elements offer comfort and continuity in a rapidly changing world.

Define your legacy by reflecting on what you want others to remember about you. Consider writing a personal letter to your descendants, sharing wisdom and experiences that have shaped you. This letter can serve as a guiding light for future generations, offering insights into your values and aspirations. Creating a family time capsule is another creative way to capture the essence of your life. Fill it with meaningful items, letters, and mementos that capture your journey and vision for the future. These tangible expressions of your legacy can be powerful reminders of your impact and intentions, inspiring a sense of purpose and motivation.

Ethical wills will offer a unique opportunity to communicate your values and life lessons. Unlike legal wills, which focus on material assets and the distribution of wealth, ethical wills convey your moral legacy. They have been utilized for centuries across various cultures and religions, serving as a bridge between generations. You might include personal reflections, guiding principles, and hopes for your descendants in an ethical will. This document provides a space for introspection and can be a profound gift to those you leave behind. It addresses mortality and clarifies life's meaning, creating a sense of symbolic immortality.

Consider engaging in legacy projects that reflect your passions and interests. Establishing a scholarship fund in a family member's name can create educational opportunities and foster growth. This act honors the individual and inspires future generations to value learning and development. Creating a family archive or genealogical record can preserve your family's history and ensure its stories are shared. These projects embody the essence of legacy planning, leaving a lasting impact beyond financial considerations.

Legacy Journaling Exercise

Take a moment to reflect on your values and the legacy you wish to leave. Write down critical aspects of your life that you want to pass on to future generations. Consider documenting family stories, traditions, and personal reflections. Use this exercise as a foundation for creating an ethical will or personal letter to your descendants. This process encourages thoughtful consideration of your legacy and offers a meaningful way to communicate your life's purpose. The 'Interactive Element: Legacy Journaling Exercise' provides a structured approach to this reflection, guiding you through the process and helping you uncover aspects of your legacy you may not have considered.

Creating a Family Mission Statement with Values and Vision

A family mission statement acts as a compass, steering the collective journey of a family through shared values and long-term goals. Its purpose is to unify family members by encapsulating the principles that define them as a unit. By articulating these shared values, a family can establish a clear vision guiding decisions and behaviors, ensuring each member feels connected to a larger purpose. This shared vision fosters a sense of identity and belonging, creating a foundation upon which family members can rely when making decisions. It serves as a reminder of what is most important: offering guidance during uncertainty and change.

Involving the whole family in creating this mission statement is crucial. You must listen to each member's input to ensure the statement accurately reflects the family's aspirations and values. Family workshops or retreats provide an ideal setting for collaboration. These gatherings allow everyone to contribute ideas and perspectives, fostering a sense of ownership and commitment to the final statement. Regular family meetings can also be instrumental in refining the mission. By revisiting the statement periodically, the family can ensure that it remains relevant and aligned with their evolving dynamics. This ongoing engagement helps maintain unity and encourages open communication, strengthening family bonds.

Aligning estate planning decisions with the family mission statement is a logical next step. By doing so, families can ensure consistency and coherence in their actions. For instance, choosing charitable causes that align with the family's values reinforces the mission and demonstrates a commitment to shared principles. Similarly, making investment decisions that support the mission can strengthen the family's financial foundation while upholding its core values. This alignment ensures that financial and philanthropic efforts are purposeful and reflect the family's collective identity. It also provides clarity and direction, helping family members make decisions that honor their shared vision.

Periodic review and revision of the family mission statement are essential to its continued relevance. As families grow and change, new members bring fresh perspectives and ideas. Incorporating feedback from these individuals can enrich the mission, ensuring that it evolves alongside the family. Adapting the statement to reflect shifting dynamics allows it to remain a living document that grows with the family. This adaptability is critical to maintaining its significance and utility over time. By regularly revisiting the mission, families can ensure that it continues to serve as a guiding light, providing direction and purpose as they navigate the complexities of life together.

Family Mission Statement Workshop

Consider organizing a family workshop to create or refine your mission statement collaboratively. Begin by gathering in a comfortable setting where everyone can share their thoughts openly. Start with a brainstorming session, encouraging each family member to express what they believe are the core values and goals of the family. Use flip charts or a whiteboard to capture ideas and facilitate discussion. Once you have a list, work together to condense these values into a cohesive statement that resonates with all members. This process strengthens family bonds and ensures the mission statement reflects the family's vision. Display the finalized statement in a common area as a reminder of your shared values and goals. The 'Interactive Element: Family Mission Statement Workshop' provides a step-by-step guide to conducting this workshop, making it easy to implement in your family.

Giving Back and Building a Legacy Through Philanthropy and Estate Planning

Philanthropy is a powerful way to extend your legacy beyond the confines of material wealth. It allows you to make a meaningful impact on society, aligning your financial resources with the causes you care deeply about. Integrating philanthropic goals into your estate plan perpetuates your values and creates a lasting impact that can endure for generations. Establishing a charitable trust or foundation is one of the most effective ways to achieve this. A charitable trust can provide a steady flow of resources to support your chosen causes while offering tax benefits.

Similarly, a family foundation allows you to manage donations strategically, realizing your philanthropic vision over time. Including bequests to favorite charities in your will is another straightforward method to support organizations that resonate with your values. These endowments can be particularly impactful, providing much-needed support to charities and allowing them to continue their work.

When selecting meaningful causes to support through your estate plan, it's essential to reflect on the issues and initiatives that resonate with you. Consider supporting local community programs that address pressing needs in your area. Doing so strengthens your community and ensures that your contributions are making a direct impact. Funding educational initiatives or scholarships is another way to create a legacy of empowerment and opportunity. By investing in education, you can help shape the future, providing individuals with the tools they need to succeed. Whether it's supporting a local school or establishing a scholarship fund, your contributions can make a significant difference in the lives of others. The key is to align your philanthropic efforts with your values, ensuring that your legacy reflects what matters most to you.

Exploring different philanthropic vehicles can maximize the effectiveness of your giving. Donor-advised funds offer flexibility, allowing you to direct your contributions to various charities over time. This option provides a structured approach to giving, enabling you to respond to changing needs and priorities. Charitable gift annuities are another option, combining income with giving. They provide you with a steady income stream during your lifetime, with the remainder going to your chosen charity. This approach benefits you financially and ensures that your resources support meaningful causes. Understanding these vehicles and their advantages can help you make informed decisions about your philanthropic strategy, enabling you to leave a legacy of generosity and impact.

Measuring and celebrating the impact of your philanthropic efforts is a crucial part of legacy planning. By tracking the progress of funded projects, you can see firsthand the difference your contributions are making. Tracking this provides a sense of accomplishment and allows you to adjust your giving strategy as needed. Organizing annual family gatherings to review philanthropic successes can be a meaningful way to involve your loved ones. These gatherings offer an opportunity to reflect on the past year's achievements, celebrate milestones, and plan for future endeavors. They also instill a sense of responsibility and commitment to philanthropy in future generations. By sharing your experiences and insights, you can inspire your family to continue your legacy of giving, ensuring that your values and vision endure.

As we conclude this chapter, it's clear that philanthropy is a vital component of a well-rounded estate plan. You can create a legacy far beyond financial assets by integrating charitable goals, selecting meaningful causes, exploring various giving vehicles, and celebrating your impact. It is not merely about giving but about creating lasting change that aligns with your values and vision. As we move forward, consider how these strategies can be integrated into your estate plan, paving the way for a legacy that reflects your life's work and aspirations. As we transition into the next chapter, we'll explore how to ensure that your estate plan remains dynamic and compelling, adapting to life's inevitable changes and challenges.

Conclusion

A s we conclude this journey through estate planning, let's revisit the core concepts that have guided us. We've explored the fundamentals of living trusts, strategies to protect your assets, and the importance of personalized planning. We delved into how technology can aid in streamlining your estate management and the crucial role of professional advice in ensuring your plans are legally sound and practical.

Throughout this book, the focus has been empowering you to control your financial future. The lessons provide actionable steps you can implement to secure your legacy. Regularly updating your estate plan is paramount as life and your plans change. This ongoing engagement is critical to ensuring your plan remains relevant and practical. Avoiding common pitfalls can save your estate from unnecessary complications, and leveraging digital tools can increase efficiency and clarity.

Estate planning is an empowering process. It is not merely about distributing assets but about securing peace of mind for you and your loved ones. It allows you to align your financial decisions with your values, ensuring that your legacy reflects what matters most to you. Taking control of this process will enable you to provide security and clarity for those you care about, creating a lasting impact.

Now is the time to take action. Whether you are just beginning your estate planning journey or revisiting an existing plan, the steps you take today will make a significant difference. Set specific goals for your estate plan, consult professionals to navigate the complexities, and utilize the tools and strategies discussed in this book. Your diligence now will prevent potential challenges in the future.

I understand that estate planning can seem daunting. Concerns about legal intricacies or the fear of making mistakes are common. However, overcoming these challenges with the proper guidance and resources will simplify the handling of your estate. It's okay to seek professional help. Trust in the process, and remember that every step you take is toward securing a brighter future for yourself and your family.

I encourage you to continue engaging with the topic of estate planning. Seek out additional resources such as estate planning forums where you can learn from others' experiences. Consider attending workshops to deepen your understanding or connecting with professionals who can provide personalized advice tailored to your needs. Also, don't hesitate to share your journey with your loved ones. Open communication about your estate plan can foster understanding and peace of mind for all involved.

As your guide on this journey, I am grateful for your trust and dedication to considering your legacy and the well-being of your loved ones. Your proactive approach to estate planning reflects your commitment to your peace of mind and the security of future generations; it demonstrates your empowerment and control over your financial future. The insights in this book have equipped you with the knowledge and confidence to navigate the path ahead.

Estate planning is a positive and rewarding process. It is an opportunity to honor your values and aspirations, secure your assets, and preserve the essence of who you are. Embrace this process to create a meaningful impact that extends beyond your lifetime. As you progress, may you find joy in knowing you have taken steps to protect what you hold dear and in the potential you have to make a significant and lasting impact.

Thank you for allowing me to join your estate planning journey. Your commitment to this vital task is commendable; it is integral. I am confident that you will achieve the peace and security you seek. As you continue on this path, remember that your legacy is not just about what you leave behind but about the lives you touch.

For more people to benefit from the information in this book, they need your help. If this book was informative and of use to you, please leave an honest review to help others recognize this resource.

Thank you,
George Munson

Glossary

- **Administrator**
  A person appointed by the court to manage and distribute the estate of someone who dies without a will (intestate).

- **Beneficiary**
  An individual or entity named in a will, trust, or other estate planning document to receive assets or benefits.

- **Codicil**
  A legal document that amends, adds to, or revokes parts of an existing will without rewriting the entire document.

- **Decedent**
  A legal term for a person who has passed away.

- **Durable Power of Attorney**
  A document granting someone the authority to make financial or legal decisions on another's behalf, even if the person becomes incapacitated.

- **Estate**
  All the assets and liabilities a person owns at the time of their death.

- **Executor**
  An individual named in a will to administer and distribute the estate according to the terms of the will.

- **Fiduciary**
  A person or institution legally bound to act in the best interests of another, such as a trustee or executor.

- **Grantor**
  The person who creates a trust, transferring assets into it for the benefit of beneficiaries.

- **Heir**
  A person legally entitled to inherit property under state intestacy laws if there is no will.

- **Intestate**
  Dying without a valid will, leading to the distribution of assets according to state laws.

- **Irrevocable Trust**
  A trust that cannot be modified or terminated by the grantor after its creation, except under specific circumstances.

- **Joint Tenancy**
  A form of property ownership by two or more people with rights of survivorship, meaning the property passes to the surviving owner(s) automatically.

- **Living Trust**
  A trust created during a person's lifetime to manage their assets and simplify distribution after death, potentially avoiding probate.

- **Living Will**
  A document specifying a person's medical treatment preferences if they cannot communicate their wishes.

- **Per Stirpes**
  A method of distributing an estate where descendants inherit their deceased parent's share equally.

- **Probate**
  The legal process of validating a will, settling debts, and distributing the estate of a deceased person.

- **Revocable Trust**
  A trust that can be altered or revoked by the grantor during their lifetime.

- **Testator**
  A person who creates and signs a will.

- **Trustee**
  An individual or institution responsible for managing assets held in a trust according to its terms.

References

- *Estate Planning Articles - Learn Center | Trust & Will.* (n.d.). Trust & Will. https://trustandwill.com/learn/estate-planning

- *Write your legal will online, free & simple | FreeWill.* (n.d.). FreeWill. https://www.freewill.com/learn/estate-planning-101

- *Estate Planning Guide.* (n.d.). https://smartasset.com/estate-planning

- *Estate planning.* (n.d.). NCOA Adviser. https://www.ncoa.org/adviser/estate-planning/

- Bieber, C., JD. (2024, November 28). *Revocable vs. irrevocable trusts: differences, pros and cons.* Forbes Advisor. https://www.forbes.com/advisor/legal/estate-law/revocable-vs-irrevocable-trust/

- *Choosing the right trustee - fiduciary trust.* (2024, May 9). Fiduciary Trust. https://www.fiduciary-trust.com/insights/choosing-the-right-trustee/

- The American College of Trust and Estate Counsel. (2024, November 18). *Estate Planning FAQs | Estate Planning Answers.* https://www.actec.org/estate-planning-essentials/

- *Estate planning in Louisville, KY | Lowman Law.*

(2024, August 15). The Lohman Law Offices, PSC. https://lohmanlaw.com/estate-planning/

- *Massachusetts Medical Society: Important differences between health care proxies and living wills.* (n.d.). https://www.massmed.org/Patient-Care/Health-Topics/Health -Care-Proxies-and-End-of-Life-Care/Important-Differences-Bet ween-Health-Care-Proxies-and-Living-Wills/#:~:text=A%20Hea lth%20Care%20Proxy%20designates,to%20make%20your%20o wn%20decisions

- *Estate Planning | Britannica Money.* (n.d.). https://www.britannica.com/money/browse/Estate-Planning

- *Trust and Estate Planning in Minneapolis & St. Paul MN | Financial Advisors.* (2024, August 2). Accounting & CPA Firm Minneapolis - Tax Preparation Services St. Paul, MN. https://jakcpa.com/services/estate-and-trust/

- Ameriprise Financial. (n.d.). *Estate Planning Basics.* https://www.ameriprise.com/financial-goals-priorities/family-es tate

- Edward Jones. (n.d.). *Common questions about estate planning.* https://www.edwardjones.com/us-en/investment-services/trust-company/common-estate-planning-questions

- *Estate Planning | LegalZoom.* (2024, December 2). https://www.legalzoom.com/articles/estate-planning

www.ingramcontent.com/pod-product-compliance
Lightning Source LLC
Chambersburg PA
CBHW070335130626
46556CB00007B/2869